P9-CQI-809

BATTLES
THAT CHANGED THE WORLD

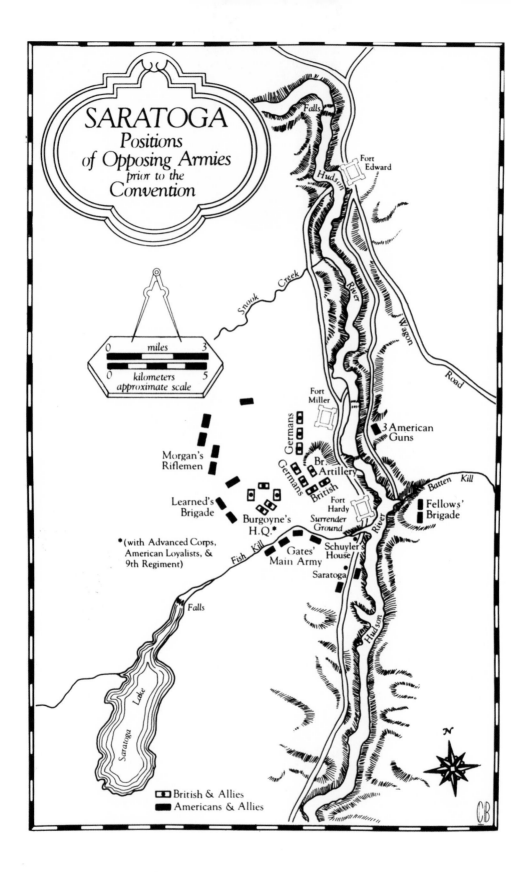

SARATOGA
Positions
of Opposing Armies
prior to the
Convention

Falls

Fort Edward

Hudson

Snook Creek

Wagon Road

0 miles 3
0 kilometers 5
approximate scale

Fort Miller

Germans

3 American Guns

Morgan's Riflemen

Germans

Br. Artillery

British

Batten Kill

Learned's Brigade

Fort Hardy

Fellows' Brigade

Burgoyne's H.Q.*

Surrender Ground

*(with Advanced Corps, American Loyalists, & 9th Regiment)

Fish Kill

Gates' Main Army

Schuyler's House

Saratoga

Falls

Hudson River

Saratoga Lake

N

British & Allies
Americans & Allies

CB

SARATOGA

RICHARD WORTH

CHELSEA HOUSE PUBLISHERS
PHILADELPHIA

Frontispiece: This map of Saratoga s   s of the American and British armies
during the battle. The British were   red by the Americans, and had no
possible avenue of escape.

CHELSEA HOUSE PUBLISHERS

EDITOR IN CHIEF Sally Cheney
DIRECTOR OF PRODUCTION Kim Shinners
CREATIVE MANAGER Takeshi Takahashi
MANUFACTURING MANAGER Diann Grasse

STAFF FOR SARATOGA

EDITOR Lee Marcott
ASSOCIATE EDITOR Bill Conn
PICTURE RESEARCHER Pat Burns
PRODUCTION ASSISTANT Jaimie Winkler
COVER AND SERIES DESIGNER Keith Trego
LAYOUT 21st Century Publishing and Communications, Inc.

http://www.chelseahouse.com

First Printing

1 3 5 7 9 8 6 4 2

Library of Congress Cataloging-in-Publication Data

Worth, Richard.
  Saratoga / Richard Worth.
    p. cm. — (Battles that changed the world)
Summary: Provides a historical account of the Revolutionary War campaign of Saratoga.
Includes bibliographical references (p.   ) and index.
  ISBN 0-7910-6682-7
  1. Saratoga Campaign, 1777—Juvenile literature. [1. Saratoga Campaign, 1777. 2. United
States—History—Revolution, 1775–1783—Campaigns.] I. Title. II. Series.
E241.S2 W67 2002
973.3'33—dc21
                                                                              2002002138

CONTENTS

Death in the Forest

General John Burgoyne led an army of more than 7,000 soldiers during his invasion of New York. Burgoyne also enlisted the aid of hundreds of Native American allies, who served as scouts and formed raiding parties designed to terrorize American settlements.

The northern shores of Lake Champlain echoed with the sound of fifes and drums as the British army set sail southward on June 20, 1777. Commanded by General John Burgoyne, the army was heading for the American stronghold at Albany in an attempt to divide the northern colonies in half, isolate New England from New York, and stamp out the American rebellion.

General Burgoyne's army of more than 7,000 soldiers, one of the largest forces ever seen in North America, created a magnificent spectacle as it traveled along Lake Champlain. The army included British regulars dressed in scarlet uniforms as well as German mercenaries in dark blue. The Hessians, as the German mercenaries were called, came from the kingdoms of Brunswick and Hesse in central Europe. They wore distinctive tall helmets decorated with polished metal insignias. In addition, there were Loyalist troops—colonists who had remained loyal to England when the revolution began. The army traveled in wide boats called bateaux, which carried 30 or 40 men as well as the large number of artillery pieces that accompanied the soldiers. Since there were few roads in the north, the only way for a large army to advance over long distances was by water. They intended to sail along Lake Champlain, over a short land route to Lake George, then down the Hudson River to Albany.

Burgoyne was also joined by approximately 500 Native American allies, who acted as scouts for the army and went on raiding parties designed to terrorize the American settlements. Among the Native Americans were heavily painted warriors from the Wyandot, Ottawa, and Ojibwa tribes of the Great Lakes as well as the Iroquois nations from western New York.

Before setting sail down the lake, Burgoyne had issued a proclamation to the Indians. "Warriors, you are free—go forth in might and valor of your cause—strike at the common enemies . . . disturbers of public order, peace and happiness, destroyers of commerce [and the] state." As one historian has written, this seemed like an open invitation to the Native Americans to engage in bloody warfare across the frontier. But Burgoyne added: "I positively forbid bloodshed when you are not opposed in arms. Aged men, women, children and prisoners must be held sacred from the knife or hatchet, even in actual conflict."

Unfortunately, many women and children found themselves in harm's way and lost their lives, and their scalps, as Burgoyne's army marched southward. The British general reportedly offered bounties, or money, for every scalp brought in by an Indian warrior. But he may not have needed to offer any reward. Many of the Native American tribes were determined to drive the American settlers back to the Atlantic coast to preserve tribal hunting grounds from being destroyed. For Burgoyne, the purpose of the Indian raids was to frighten colonials who might be thinking of joining the American army and persuade them to stay at home and sit out the war. However, Burgoyne's plan had the reverse effect, largely due to a single incident involving a young woman named Jane McCrea.

Born in New Jersey, Jane was one of seven children of a Presbyterian minister in Jersey City. Her mother died when she was still a child, and after her father's death, Jane moved to New York to live with her brother John who had settled along the Hudson River near Albany. After the American Revolution broke out in 1775, John joined up with the American army. However, Jane had fallen in love with a young man named David Jones, who had enlisted in Burgoyne's army—so, she was torn between her loyalties to the Americans and the British. At first, Jane followed her brother. But as news of the British army's advance reached her, she decided to move in with a woman named Mrs. McNeil who lived in the path of Burgoyne's advancing force. Mrs. McNeil was well known to the British because she was the cousin of one of Burgoyne's commanders. By staying with Mrs. McNeil, Jane may have hoped to see Jones, who was now a captain in the British army.

Jane McCrea was reportedly a strikingly beautiful young woman, with long reddish hair that streamed down her back and may have even touched the floor. During July, as the British advanced southward, Jane and

Mrs. McNeil remained in their house with a black female servant and two small children. Unfortunately, the house became the target of a Native American attack. As the Indians approached, Jane, Mrs. McNeil, the servant, and the children tried to hide in a cellar underneath a separate part of the house. While the servant and children were able to hide undetected, the Indians caught up with Jane and Mrs. McNeil before they could find shelter. Two Indians dragged them away.

Meanwhile, someone had brought news of the Native American attack to a group of American militiamen stationed at a nearby fort. They began to pursue the Indians. As the militia caught sight of them, shots were exchanged. One of the soldiers was captured, and the Native Americans escaped with the two women and the soldier. However, according to the soldier, an argument began between the Indians over Jane McCrea. As the soldier later reported: "In the midst of the fray, one of the Chiefs in a rage shot . . . McCrea in her breast, & she fell & expired immediately. Her hair was long and flowing, and the same chief took off the scalp, cutting so as to unbrace nearly the whole of that part of the head on which the hair grew."

The Indian, named Panther, showed up at Burgoyne's camp, carrying Jane McCrea's scalp. As he displayed the trophy, David Jones recognized his loved-one's hair immediately. He was horrified and greatly saddened by her murder. General Burgoyne was also stunned and wanted Panther executed immediately. However, the Native American warrior claimed that he had not killed McCrea. He said that a stray bullet had accidentally hit her during the battle with the American militia. Whatever was the true story, Burgoyne finally let Panther off with a reprimand. The general was afraid that all his Indian allies might desert if Panther was

The death of Jane McCrea at the hands of General Burgoyne's Native American allies angered many Americans, who then joined General Gates to fight the British.

executed, and the British might lose valuable scouts.

Nevertheless, the incident was not over. Because of the cruelty of McCrea's death, Burgoyne felt he owed an explanation to the American commanding general, Horatio Gates. Burgoyne did not want the Americans to believe that the British were waging war on innocent women and children. As Burgoyne wrote: "The fact was no premeditated barbarity. On the contrary, two chiefs who had brought her off for the purposes of security, not of violence to her person, disputed which should be her guard; and in a fit of savage passion in the one from whose hands she was snatched, the unhappy woman became the victim."

General Gates, however, refused to accept Burgoyne's explanation. As Gates put it: "The miserable fate of Miss McCrea was particularly aggravated by her being dressed up to receive her promised husband, but met her murderer employed by you." General Gates's letter was reprinted throughout New England. In addition, the story of Jane McCrea was published in a variety of newspapers in New York and Massachusetts, as well as in Pennsylvania, Maryland, and Virginia.

While other settlers had been murdered on the frontier, the death of Jane McCrea seemed to capture the attention of many more Americans. Perhaps it was because she had been so beautiful. She was also engaged to marry one of Burgoyne's own officers. If the British could not even protect their own supporters from the Indians, people reasoned, then no one was safe on the frontier.

The murder of Jane McCrea had an instant impact across New York and New England. Hundreds of militiamen left their homes to join General Gates's army that was opposing the British invasion of New York. Eventually, the American forces would far outnumber the invaders, which had a decisive effect on the battles around

Saratoga, New York, that would be fought in September and October 1777.

As one historian explained: "If the Battle of Saratoga was the turning point of the American Revolution, the death of Jane McCrea might rightly be argued as the turning point of that battle."

Opening Battles

Marquis de Montcalm, the French commanding general, died during the Battle of Quebec in 1759. The British army's decisive victory over the French in this battle eliminated the threat of future French invasions. However, it also gave the British army strongholds from which to attack the Americans at the beginning of the Revolutionary War.

The Saratoga campaign of 1777 was part of a continuing back-and-forth struggle for the Hudson River Valley, considered Canada's gateway into New York and New England. The battle for the valley had begun much earlier between France and Great Britain, who were involved in a long conflict for power on the North American continent.

French explorers established settlements in Canada during the 17th century. Quebec, located on the St. Lawrence River, became the capital of New France. Montreal, farther inland along the river, developed into a successful trading center. From Montreal, French trappers set out into the wilderness to hunt beaver and trade with the Indian tribes along the Great Lakes for beaver pelts. These pelts were part of a profitable trade with Europe, where they were manufactured into fur hats, coats, and other garments.

To protect their trade and their empire, the French established outposts, or forts, along the Great Lakes and the Ohio River valley, as well as in northern New York. In 1726, France built a fort called St. Frederic on Lake Champlain. And in 1755, the French began erecting a large stone structure called Carillon at the base of Lake Champlain. No army could invade New France from the south without first capturing Carillon and St. Frederic. From these forts, however, the French could, and did, send their own troops and Native American allies in raids against English settlements.

To counter the French positions, the English established their own trading posts and fortified positions in North America. Although the Dutch had originally founded New York, the colony fell to the English after a brief war in the 17th century. Albany, on the Hudson River, became a successful fur trading post. The English established close relations with the Iroquois Indians, whose villages lay in western New York State. With the permission of the Iroquois, the English established a fortified post on Lake Ontario, called Oswego, during the 1720s. Later, in 1755, the British also built Fort William Henry at the base of Lake George to protect Albany from possible capture by an invading French force.

By this time, France and England were engaged in a titanic struggle for control of North America—the French and Indian War—part of a worldwide conflict called the Seven Years War. France won the early battles. In 1756, a French army under the Marquis de Montcalm destroyed Oswego, and the following year Montcalm captured Fort William Henry. But the English, relying on superior manpower and a better fleet, finally prevailed. In 1759, an army commanded by General Jeffrey Amherst captured forts Carillon and St. Frederic, renaming them Ticonderoga and Crown Point. Quebec fell to a British army led by General James Wolfe, and Montreal was captured in 1760.

The English settlers could now rest easy because the threat from New France had finally ended. But in 1775, as the American Revolution began, these same settlers faced a new threat. The British might invade New York from Canada, following the same route along Lake Champlain and Lake George that Montcalm had traveled in 1757. America's political leaders decided that the best way to prevent such an invasion was to seize Fort Ticonderoga, called "the key to the gateway to the continent."

Two very different men shared command of the American forces. One of them, Ethan Allen, was a tall, powerful backwoodsman from Vermont who led a group of militia called the Green Mountain Boys. The other commander was Captain Benedict Arnold, who had been a successful merchant in Connecticut before the outbreak of the war. During the dark morning hours of May 10, 1775, Allen and Arnold led a small force against Fort Ticonderoga. The fort had been allowed to deteriorate since the French and Indian War, as there was no longer any threat from New France. In addition, only a small force of British soldiers manned Ticonderoga. The American force took the British completely by surprise and easily captured Fort Ticonderoga. But Arnold and Allen were not content with a single victory. They headed northward, surprising the British garrison at Crown Point, and capturing this post, too.

Ethan Allen believed that the only way to end the threat of British invasion was to lead an American force into Canada, capture Montreal and Quebec, and win over

Ethan Allen is depicted here, leading the raid on Fort Ticonderoga in 1775. The American forces, led by Allen and Benedict Arnold, also captured Crown Point.

the support of the French Canadians. As he put it: "The more vigorous the Colonies push the war against the King's Troops in Canada, the more friends we shall find in that country. . . . Should the Colonies forthwith send an army of two or three thousand men, and attack Montreal, we . . . would easily make a conquest of that place." Brigadier General Richard Montgomery, one of the American commanders in New York state, agreed. A veteran of the victories at Crown Point and Ticonderoga during the French and Indian War, Montgomery believed the key to the defense of the Hudson River lay in Canada.

Montgomery set out from Fort Ticonderoga in August to invade Canada. After a long and difficult siege, the American forces took the British outpost at St. Johns on the Richelieu River in November. By this time, winter had already begun, but Montgomery would not turn back. The British put up only a mild defense of Montreal, and it was surrendered on November 13, 1775.

Meanwhile, Benedict Arnold was leading another American force against the capital city at Quebec. Joined by Montgomery, Arnold attacked Quebec in a driving blizzard on December 31, 1775. This time the British forces, commanded by Governor-General Guy Carleton, beat back the American attack. Montgomery was killed, and Arnold severely wounded. Still, the American forces did not retreat. Arnold continued to lay siege to Quebec throughout the winter and spring of 1776. However, his supplies began to run out, and many of his men became sick with small pox.

The St. Lawrence River froze during the winter and cut off Canada from European ships. But by May, when the river thawed, Governor Carleton received reinforcements from England. Major General John Burgoyne arrived with 4,000 British troops under his command. The Americans were chased out of Montreal, and retreated with their sick and wounded down the lakes to Crown Point and Ticonderoga.

The seesaw battle for control of the north had now taken another turn. During 1775, the Americans seemed to have the upper hand. Now, in 1776, the advantage passed to

General Richard Montgomery was killed during the American attack on the British-held city of Quebec in 1775. Although the American forces led by Benedict Arnold continued to battle for the city, they were eventually driven back when British reinforcements arrived.

the British. General Carleton decided to capitalize on his advantage by invading New York and capturing Crown Point and Fort Ticonderoga.

At these two posts the American army was in terrible condition. Many of the men were sick or dying following the retreat from Canada. They had little food to eat, their clothes were in tatters, and they lacked ammunition to repel an invasion. General Philip Schuyler, who commanded the northern army, decided that his troops were too weak to hold Crown Point and decided to concentrate his forces at Fort Ticonderoga. Gradually, reinforcements began to arrive along with supplies that strengthened the American position. By the end of August 1776, there were almost 5,000 soldiers present and fit for duty.

However, foot soldiers alone would not be enough to defend Lake Champlain. Schuyler and Benedict Arnold both realized that they needed ships to command the lake and stop a British invasion. The Americans already had several schooners on the lake. One had been captured at St. Johns in 1775 and another at Ticonderoga. But these were not enough to stop Carleton who was reportedly building a powerful flotilla at the other end of the lake. Since the forests around Lake Champlain were thick with trees, Arnold set his men to work cutting timber. As a merchant, he was familiar with shipbuilding and knew how to command ships. The timber was cut using three sawmills in the area. Schuyler sent word to the New England states that he needed ship's carpenters and a few of them traveled to Lake Champlain to shape the timber into boats. They built large row galleys, which were protected by several cannon. Arnold also ordered that a few guns should be placed on the schooners.

At the same time, Carleton was building a fleet at St. Johns. He had a three-masted ship, two schooners, and a flotilla of gunboats. They carried more cannon than Arnold's ships. Carleton's army was also much stronger. It included approximately 8,000 British troops led by General Burgoyne, as well as 5,000 German soldiers under the command of Major General Baron von Riedesel.

By the end of August, Arnold's fleet was complete and began sailing northward on Lake Champlain. Since he was facing a stronger force, Arnold decided to take up a defensive position. At Valcour Island, in the northern part of Lake Champlain, he arranged his ships in an arc. They were strung across the water toward the western shore, about a half-mile away. Carleton had left St. Johns in early October with his flotilla, but they were already south of Valcour Island before spotting the American position on October 11, 1775. Once they saw the Americans, the British fleet turned and began firing on the enemy ships. As Baron von Riedesel later wrote: "A tremendous cannonade was opened on both sides."

Arnold was in one of the galleys, and led the attack on the British schooner *Carleton.* The fighting was very heavy, with Arnold's galley taking many direct hits. As Arnold later wrote: "Some of the enemy's ships . . . rowed up within musket-shot of us. They continued a very hot fire with round and grape shot [types of artillery shells] until five o'clock." Eventually, British fire power proved too much for the Americans. By nightfall, 60 men had been killed or wounded and many of their ships were heavily damaged. Arnold decided to break off the engagement and escape southward under cover of nightfall.

The next morning, when Carleton realized that the American flotilla had escaped, he pursued them. Eventually, the British caught up with Arnold's ships and began pounding them again. Arnold had no choice but to call off the battle. He directed his damaged and leaky flotilla onto the eastern shore of Lake Champlain, and, after his men had evacuated them, he burned the boats so the British could not use them.

The Battle of Valcour Island seemed like a defeat for the American army. In reality, Arnold's defense of Lake Champlain would prove vitally important to the Saratoga

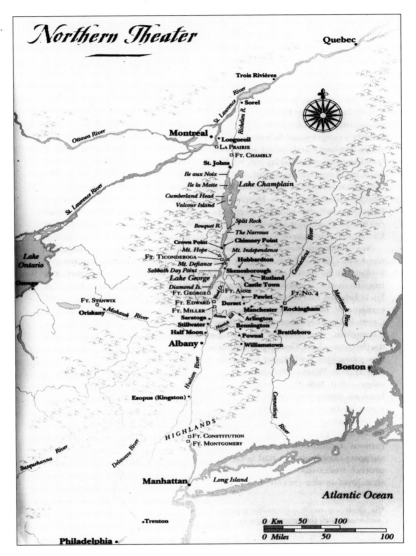

Northern Theater

Quebec

Trois Rivières

St. Lawrence River

Sorel

Montreal

Longueuil
□ LA PRAIRIE
□ FT. CHAMBLY

St. Johns

Ile aux Noix
Ile la Motte   Lake Champlain
Cumberland Head
Valcour Island

Bouquet R.
Split Rock
The Narrows
Crown Point   *Chimney Point*
Mt. Hope   *Mt. Independence*
FT. TICONDEROGA   *Hubberdton*
Mt. Defiance
Sabbath Day Point   *Skenesborough*
Lake George   *Rutland*
Diamond Is.   *Castle Town*
□FT. GEORGE   □FT. ANNE
FT. EDWARD □   *Pawlet*   FT. No. 4
FT. MILLER   *Dorset*
Saratoga   *Manchester*   *Rockingham*
Stillwater   *Arlington*
Half Moon   *Bennington*
Albany   *Pownal*   *Brattleboro*
Williamstown

FT. STANWIX □
Oriskany   *Mohawk River*

Lake
Ontario

Boston

Esopus (Kingston)

HIGHLANDS
□FT. CONSTITUTION
□ FT. MONTGOMERY

Susquehanna River   *Delaware River*   *Hudson River*   *Connecticut River*

Manhattan   *Long Island*

Atlantic Ocean

• Trenton

Philadelphia •

| 0 Km | 50 | 100 |
| 0 Miles | 50 | 100 |

In the opening years of the Revolutionary War, battles between the British and American armies occurred along the Hudson River Valley and Lake George and Lake Champlain.

campaign the following year. Since it was already so late in the year, Carleton decided not to advance toward Fort Ticonderoga. Indeed, he had been told that the Americans had 10,000 men at the fort. Leading his army against such a force in October, when winter was nearly

Colonel Benedict Arnold led a small flotilla of ships that tried to stop a British invasion at the Battle of Valcour Island in October 1775.

at hand, and beginning a siege of the fort was highly risky. Carleton might not be able to supply his army from Canada because snowy winter conditions would make travel impossible.

So Carleton decided to retreat to Canada. In fact, he did not even occupy Crown Point or leave a small garrison there for the winter. The return northward, which had been brought on because Carleton had been forced to spend several months building a fleet to oppose Arnold, meant that the British would have to begin their campaign again from Canada in 1777. This would stretch British supply lines and give the Americans time to gather an army to oppose a new invasion.

General Burgoyne, who had participated in the British invasion of 1776, disagreed with Carleton's decision to retreat to Canada without leaving a garrison at Crown Point or attempting to take Fort Ticonderoga. Burgoyne was a commander who believed in taking risks. He had fought successfully against the French in Europe where his men nicknamed him "Gentleman Johnny." They loved his boldness and regarded him as an effective commander. Burgoyne was also a playwright who hobnobbed with actors on the English stage, and he served as a member of Britain's parliament.

Most importantly, Burgoyne was a friend of Lord George Germain, Secretary of State for the Colonies, and the man in charge of propagating the war against the American rebels. After the 1776 campaign had ended, Burgoyne returned to London. His wife had recently died while he was away in Canada, and he grieved over her loss. He also wanted to meet with Germain and propose a new campaign for 1777. Both Germain and King George III believed that the war against the Americans had to be pursued forcefully, and the rebellion put down immediately.

During the summer of 1776, a British army commanded by Lord William Howe had taken control of New York City. However, Howe allowed the American army under its commander-in-chief, General George Washington, to escape. Carleton, Germain believed, had shown the same lack of initiative in not accomplishing more during his invasion of upper New York. To remedy

General John Burgoyne convinced the British government that he should command an army to invade New York and capture Albany in 1777. Lord Germain and King George III both agreed that the American rebellion had to be put down quickly.

this situation, General Burgoyne proposed a new plan of attack for 1777. It was contained in what he called his "Thoughts" on the coming campaign. Burgoyne intended that the British regain the initiative in northern New York, which he believed had been lost with Carleton's retreat.

Burgoyne wanted to gather a force of 8,000 British and

German regular troops, along with 1,000 Indians and 2,000 Canadian militias. While some of the regulars would be left to hold Canada, the rest of the army would march south taking control of Lake Champlain, capturing Fort Ticonderoga, and meeting up with the British army under Lord Howe coming northward from New York City. Meanwhile, another, smaller force would march from Canada to Lake Ontario down the Mohawk Valley, raising support from Loyalists and Indians living in the area. Thus, three giant pincers would converge on Albany, capture the city, and separate New York from New England, stamping out the rebellion.

Burgoyne, of course, expected to command the invasion from Canada. Lord Germain and King George accepted Burgoyne's plan during the winter of 1777. "Gentleman Johnny" sailed for Canada where he arrived in May, after the ice had melted and the St. Lawrence River was open to navigation. Unfortunately, no one ever made clear to Sir William Howe what his role in the campaign should be. Sir William decided that instead of cooperating with Burgoyne, he would move most of his army southward from New York for an attack on the American capital at Philadelphia. Howe also hoped to force General Washington into defending the capital city and, if possible, destroy the American army.

Therefore, Burgoyne was left on his own without any assistance from Howe. This would have an enormous impact on the outcome of the entire campaign.

Ticonderoga

The French build Fort Ticonderoga, which they called *Le Carillon,* in 1755-56 to guard the northern route to Canada along Lake Champlain.

In the cool autumn of 1755, Michel Chartier de Lotbiniere surveyed the dense forests that lay at the southern end of Lake Champlain. Lotbiniere was a Canadian, but he had studied in France, receiving extensive training as an engineer in military fortifications. At the base of Lake Champlain he hoped to lay out a massive fort to guard the northern route to Canada. The French called this fortress *Le Carillon,* the Chimes, because they thought a nearby waterfall sounded like the beautiful music of church bells.

Before construction of Carillon could begin, Canadian workmen had to clear away a large swath of dense forest. Then, using black powder, they blasted out thick stone ledges that lay in the ground. Finally, work on Fort Carillon started. The walls were over 500 feet in length and they connected four bastions at each corner that were shaped like stars. The icy northern winter prevented Lotbiniere from finishing Carillon in 1755, but work continued the next spring and through the summer. Fort Carillon included a bakery with ovens large enough to provide bread for the entire garrison, as well as barracks for officers and soldiers, a dungeon, and a powder magazine.

In the summer of 1758, during the French and Indian War, a British army of 14,000 soldiers under the command of General James Abercrombie sailed northward up Lake George to attack Fort Carillon. A French army of only 3,500 troops was defending the fort. The French commander General Marquis de Montcalm realized that he had too few soldiers to man all the battlements at the fort. Therefore, Montcalm decided to build a defensive work north of Carillon. In the hot July sun, French soldiers hastily erected a wooden breastwork. In front, they placed a massive network of sharp pointed sticks—called an abatis—designed to stop enemy soldiers before they could climb the breastwork. On the morning of July 8, 1758, the British made a frontal assault on the French position. Unaccountably, General Abercrombie did not bring up his massive artillery that could have easily destroyed the French position. Again and again, the British infantry charged across the open plateau toward the breastwork and each time they were driven back with terrible losses. Finally, Abercrombie retreated, leaving almost 2,000 of his men dead or wounded on the field. The French had won a miraculous victory. As Montcalm later wrote: "If ever troops were worthy of reward it has been those that I have the honor to command."

A year later, the French had fallen back on Quebec, which was being besieged by a large British army. Another force of 11,000 men, commanded by General Jeffrey Amherst, advanced against Fort Carillon. This time the French were not strong enough to hold their position, and they retreated. But before leaving, they laid powder charges around the fort. As one historian wrote, on the evening of July 26, 1759, there "was a swelling roar. A bright pillar of flame stabbed high into the night sky and every corner and angle of Lotbiniere's great work was outlined sharply against the lake. Men saw great masses of masonry tossed about like chips in a flood while the very ground shook and trembled. . . . The fire burned on through the night. Dull crashes sounded as solid beams collapsed under the weight they supported."

The French had destroyed part of the fort, which the British occupied and renamed Ticonderoga—an Indian word that means "land between the waters." But the fort remained in a state of disrepair until the Americans captured it in 1775. Two years later, as General Burgoyne's army descended upon Lake Champlain, the American army scrambled to defend the fort against the British army. The defenses were still inadequate. In addition, the American army numbered only about 2,500 men—too few to adequately man the walls.

The American forces were commanded by Major General Arthur St. Clair (pronounced *Sinclair*). A veteran of the French and Indian War, St. Clair had also commanded troops during the early fighting of the American Revolution. As St. Clair surveyed his forces, he realized that they were a mixed collection of troops. Some regiments were Continentals—men who had enlisted for the duration of the war. While a small number of these Continentals had seen action during the Revolution, others were still untrained. In addition,

Military Equipment of Continental Soldiers

Many of the American soldiers were experienced hunters. Part of their uniform was a long hunting shirt made out of cloth or deer leather, with fringe on the sleeves. The shirt was originally supposed to be worn around camp. But soldiers often wore the shirt in battle, because it was the only shirt they owned. The Continental army in 1777 could not afford to issue standard uniforms to its troops. Unlike the British or German troops who were smartly dressed in splendid uniforms, the American soldiers often wore what they had brought with them from home.

In addition to a hunting shirt, the continental infantryman wore a tri-corned hat. The men also wore knee-length breeches or overalls as well as boots or shoes. Today, we are used to having shoes fitted to our right and left feet. During the colonial period, both shoes were identical. A smart soldier might shift the shoes or boots back and forth from one foot to the other to reduce wear. Buckles and straps kept the shoes from falling of a soldier's foot. Frequently, the shoes were not too well fitted.

Each member of a state militia carried a musket. A favorite musket was the so-called Brown Bess. This was the same musket used by the British soldiers. Infantrymen were taught to load and shoot a musket every fifteen seconds to produce maximum fire power against the enemy. The musket shot a large lead ball. The ball could be combined with a load of powder and wrapped in a brown paper cartridge. The cartridges were kept dry in cartridge boxes carried by Continental soldiers. The cartridge box hung at the soldier's waist. If the cartridges became wet, the powder would need to be dried before the ammunition could be used in battle.

To fire a musket, the soldier shook powder into the pan of his musket at the rear of the weapon. A charge was then rammed down the musket with a ramrod. Then the infantryman took aim and fired. The muskets were accurate over a distance of up to 100 yards.

On the march, soldiers had to carry rations with them. Wooden or tin canteens contained water. A soldier's food rations might be kept in a haversack, slung over his shoulder. The rations often consisted of a small amount of beef as well as flour to make bread. Cooking was done in heavy cast iron kettles over a campfire.

St. Clair commanded two regiments of militia. The militias were untrained farmers and shopkeepers who could only be depended on to remain with the army for short periods. When they grew tired of military service, they would return home to their regular jobs. The militia often panicked at the first sight of battle, but some of them were skilled marksmen who might prove valuable in an upcoming fight.

In addition to his small military force, St. Clair had only a short supply of food and ammunition for his men. All they could hope to do was delay Burgoyne's superior army, then retreat southward. Instead of keeping his entire army inside the fort, St. Clair posted some of them on two outlying positions. One of these was located on Mount Hope, west of Fort Ticonderoga. Here the Americans had placed artillery to fire down on the advancing British. South of the fort were South Bay and Wood Creek. On the eastern side of South Bay rose Rattlesnake Hill, where the Americans had also built defenses and placed cannon. A third hill, called Mt. Defiance, lay south of Fort Ticonderoga and across a gorge that connected Lake Champlain and Lake George. However, the American commanders had put no defenses on this hill because they believed that it was far too difficult for an advancing army to climb.

On July 1, 1777, as Burgoyne advanced down Lake Champlain and neared Fort Ticonderoga, he split his army. The British marched along the western side of the lake, while the German soldiers moved along the eastern shore. Burgoyne intended to attack the fort from two different directions and prevent the American army from retreating. In command of the British troops was General Simon Fraser, 48 years old, and a veteran officer who had fought at Quebec during the French and Indian War. As Fraser's soldiers approached Mount

General Simon Fraser, a veteran British officer, served valiantly throughout the entire British invasion of 1777. He recognized that Mt. Defiance held the key to the capture of Fort Ticonderoga.

Hope, the American troops decided to abandon their position, burn it, and retreat towards Fort Ticonderoga. As they retreated, the Americans took cover behind the old French breastworks, where Indians attacked them. However, they beat back the Indian attack without suffering any casualties.

Meanwhile, Fraser saw that Mount Defiance, across the gorge from the fort, had a commanding view of Ticonderoga. He sent one of his engineers, Lieutenant

William Twiss, to find out if he could climb the hill. Twiss returned several hours later and reported that a road might be built so artillery could be wheeled to the top of the mountain. As one of Fraser's officers put it: "Where a goat can go, a man can go and where a man can go he can drag a gun." From this position the British could fire their guns down into Fort Ticonderoga, forcing the Americans to abandon it. On July 4, the British soldiers started building a narrow, dirt road up the mountain. By noon of the following day, they were positioning artillery on the summit.

When General St. Clair realized what the British had accomplished, he knew that the American position inside Fort Ticonderoga had become indefensible. He decided immediately to retreat. Fortunately, the German army commanded by Baron von Riedesel, which was making its way around behind Fort Ticonderoga from the east, had not reached its final position. St. Clair's troops still had time to make their escape. But General St. Clair realized how difficult a task lay before him. As he put it, "a retreat, with an inferior army, from before a superior one, is perhaps the most delicate and dangerous undertaking in the whole circle of military operations." St. Clair meant that if the smaller army is caught while retreating and not ready for battle, the large force could easily destroy it.

Nevertheless, St. Clair had no other choice. Under the cover of darkness on the night of July 5, part of his force embarked on ships to sail southward toward Skenesboro on Wood Creek. The other part of the army crossed over the bridge from Fort Ticonderoga to the eastern shore to march to Hubbardton and Castleton. During the night, as the American troops retreated, their plan was almost revealed when the encampment on Rattlesnake Hill was mistakenly blown up by one of the American commanders. The British, however, seemed unaware of the movements by the American forces. However, it was a difficult maneuver for St. Clair and his troops, many of whom were inexperienced militia. Trying to retreat in the darkness, when no one could be sure of their footing and when the British might have attacked at any moment, was enough to cause complete panic among the troops. St. Clair and his commanders kept most of the men calm. By the following morning they had made their escape, and Burgoyne was surprised to discover that Ticonderoga had been completely abandoned.

Immediately, he sent General Fraser southward to Hubbardton in pursuit of the Americans. Burgoyne, himself, destroyed the bridge across Lake Champlain so his ships could sail from Lake Champlain, past Ticonderoga and pursue the American contingent heading toward Skenesboro. St. Clair made a rapid retreat to Hubbardtown. There he left a contingent under the command of Colonel Seth Warner to delay the British advance until the American forces could reach Castleton and eventually rendezvous with the rest of their troops at Skenesboro.

Since Warner's men had endured a long, hot march to Hubbardtown, he decided to let them rest. On the night of July 6, he put out no pickets to warn his troops of an advancing enemy. Unknown to the Americans, General Fraser was driving his men relentlessly forward. Although he let his men rest for a few hours, they were on the road again by 3:00 A.M. on July 7. By daylight, they were approaching the American camp. Fraser's scouts went ahead and reconnoitered the American position. When they came back, Fraser realized he had an opportunity to surprise the Americans.

At approximately 7:00 A.M., a shout went up from

the American camp: "The enemy are upon us." Fraser's men charged the center of the American position, while another contingent of British troops tried to outflank the American left wing. At first, the British were successful. The American position was forced to retreat. Meanwhile, a force of American troops on the right pushed back the British left, jeopardizing Fraser's position. But, before the Americans could defeat this part of the British line, reinforcements led by Baron von Riedesel and his German soldiers appeared. They had been marching behind Fraser's soldiers, and von Riedesel realized that the battle would be lost unless he reinforced the British left flank quickly. The Germans swung into line and began firing, forcing the Americans to retreat towards Castleton after losing almost half their men.

While Fraser was engaged with the enemy at Hubbardtown, Burgoyne was sailing southward with his troops toward Skenesboro. Colonel Pierce Long, commanding the American forces, had enough time to burn the fort at Skenesboro as well as several ships before Burgoyne arrived. The British had advanced far more quickly than Long had anticipated. He was forced to retreat hastily, and the British captured some of his ships as well as a large portion of his food supplies. Meanwhile, Long headed south toward Fort Anne. Burgoyne sent Lt. Colonel John Hill after Long with orders to intercept him. As Hill approached Fort Anne through a narrow heavily wooded area, Long was waiting to ambush him. When the firing started on the morning of July 8, both sides tried to gain the advantage. The British held a position on a ridge, but the American troops were slowly advancing against them. Suddenly, a war whoop went up in the rear. Indians were arriving to assist the British. Fearing himself outnumbered, Long decided to retreat. As it

The American forces fighting under Pierce Long in 1777 retreated, and burned Fort Anne to be sure it would not fall to the British. Long's men received exaggerated reports about the size of the British force they were to battle.

turned out, there were no Indians, but only a single British officer named John Money. He had been leading a group of Indians, but when they seemed reluctant to fight the Americans, Money became impatient and ran ahead of them. His war whoop had won the battle.

Inside Fort Anne, the American forces received word that the British were advancing with a much larger force. Therefore, they decided to burn the fort and retreat southward to Fort Edward. General Burgoyne, however, seemed to be in no hurry to push his advantage. Instead, he established his headquarters at Skenesboro and waited there for supplies. The supply route from Canada was getting longer and longer as Burgoyne moved farther south, so it would take many days for additional food and ammunition to arrive for the British and German troops.

Meanwhile, General Schuyler had ridden north from his headquarters at Albany to take command of the troops at Fort Edward. By mid-July there were almost 3,000 Continentals and 1,600 militia. St. Clair's men had arrived after their retreat from Ticonderoga, along with Colonel Long's contingent and additional reinforcements. However, Schuyler realized that he was not strong enough to stop Burgoyne. The best he could do was to delay him while waiting for more men to join the American army and establish a strong position farther south where he could fight Burgoyne on an equal footing.

To delay Burgoyne's advance from Skenesboro, Schuyler ordered his men to destroy the road and bridges through the woods and swamps leading from Fort Anne to Fort Edward. Schuyler also told all the farmers in the area to destroy their crops and livestock so the enemy would not have any additional food supplies. Schuyler's men did such a good job of obstructing the road that Burgoyne had to send out his own men to build a new one. As a result, his army did not reach Fort Edward until July 29. By that time, Schuyler had gone south to Saratoga.

Burgoyne's troops were elated. They had captured Fort Ticonderoga and driven the enemy southward.

General Philip Schuyler led the American defense of the Hudson River Valley against the attack by the British army. Schuyler and his men delayed the advancing British army on their march to Ft. Edward by destroying roads and bridges.

Now, at Fort Edward, they were only a few miles from the Hudson River and the route to Albany. Victory seemed within their grasp. But in early August, Burgoyne had received a message from General Howe. It said: "My intention is for Pennsylvania, where I expect to meet Washington." Burgoyne and his army were on their own. They could expect no help from General Howe who was leading his troops in the opposite direction, toward the American capital at Philadelphia. With his lengthening supply line, Burgoyne must engage the American army in battle and defeat it while he still had enough food and ammunition to supply his soldiers. But time was beginning to run out.

General John Stark, a veteran of the French and Indian War, commanded American troops at the Battle of Bennington in 1777.

John Stark and the Battle of Bennington

John Stark was a proud, powerfully-built soldier from London-derry, Vermont. Stark had been battle-tested during the French and Indian War when he served as a captain with Robert Rogers' Rangers. The Rangers were a unit of scouts attached to the British army. They knew how to hide themselves in the dense forests, steal up on an enemy position such as Fort St. Frederic or Fort Carillon, and report on its strength to the British commanders. The Rangers were also experts at ambushing French and Indian war parties. In January 1757, for example, Stark along with Rogers and his Rangers intercepted a sled carrying French soldiers that was gliding along the ice on Lake Champlain. Unfortunately, a larger unit of French troops spotted the Rangers. Rogers and his men tried to escape but they were surrounded. Rogers, himself, was wounded and Stark had to lead the rangers to safety. He discovered a secure position for the night, but fearing the rangers might be eventually overwhelmed, he went for help. Stark traveled 40 miles on snow shoes, arriving at a large British outpost the next morning. He secured sleighs to carry off the wounded rangers and brought reinforcements to save his men.

Stark left the army at the end of the war and settled in Derryfield, New Hampshire. But after the Revolutionary War broke out in 1775, he joined the American forces. As a colonel, he commanded a regiment on the front lines at the Battle of Bunker Hill in 1775. The following year, Stark participated in the American victory at Trenton. For his outstanding service, Stark expected to be promoted to general. But he was overlooked by the American Continental Congress, which was running the war, and other men were promoted ahead of him. Stark was so angry that he resigned from the American army.

As Burgoyne's army headed south in the summer of 1777, he seemed to threaten not only New York, but Vermont and New Hampshire, which lay to the east of the Hudson River. Indeed, the British general had thought about leading an army eastward and putting down the rebellion in the New England states. When Fort Ticonderoga fell to the British, northern New England felt especially threatened by Burgoyne's army. Shortly afterward, John Langdon, the Speaker of the New Hampshire legislature, rose and offered to bankroll an army. "I have a thousand dollars in hard money," he said. "I will pledge my plate [silver dinner dishes] for three thousand more. . . . They are at the service of the state. If we succeed in defending our firesides and our homes I may be remunerated; if we do not then the property will be of no value to me. Our friend, John Stark, who so nobly maintained the honor of our state at Bunker Hill, may safely be entrusted with the honor of the enterprise and we will check the progress of Burgoyne."

Stark was made a Brigadier General and began to raise an army. His reputation was so widely respected throughout New Hampshire that 1,500 men joined him in only a few days. On July 30, 1777, General Stark marched eastward to Manchester, Vermont, where he joined Colonel Seth Warner, who had retreated with his men from Hubbardton. In the meantime, General Schuyler sent word to Stark that he should continue to march to New York to meet up with the main part of the American army. Schuyler wanted as many men as possible to resist Burgoyne.

Stark refused. As he put it, his job was to defend New Hampshire and Vermont. In addition, he did not want to serve in the regular American army. He begged not to be put "under the Command of those officers on whose account I quitted the army. Lest the remedy should prove worse to me than the disease." Instead, on August 8, Stark led his army to Bennington, in southern Vermont. This was an important American supply center with food and horses for the army.

Although Stark did not know it, a force of German soldiers was also heading for Bennington. Baron von Riedesel had suggested to General Burgoyne that a small detachment might be sent eastward into Vermont to try to round up horses and supplies for the army. There were already too few horses for the cavalry, and the supply line from Canada was being stretched to the breaking point. General von Riedesel reasoned that the rich farmland in Vermont might provide the army with what they needed.

German soldiers like this regiment, along with Tories and Indians under the command of General Baum, marched to Bennington to capture horses and supplies for General Burgoyne's army.

Burgoyne agreed. But instead of a small foraging party, he decided to send a much larger force. Burgoyne hoped to protect his left flank as he marched southward, and induce Tories in Vermont to join the army. To lead the force, he chose Lieutenant Colonel Friedrich Baum. Colonel Baum commanded a small army of over 600 men, including German soldiers, Tories, and Indians. Unfortunately, Baum could not speak any English. How Burgoyne expected him to communicate with American Tories in Vermont and persuade them to enlist in the army was unclear. Shortly before Baum began his march eastward, Burgoyne changed his orders. Baum was to take his army to Bennington and capture the American supplies. Although they did not know it, Baum and Stark were now on a collision course.

As Baum headed toward Bennington, the Indian warriors with him looted the countryside and frightened the local farmers. Stark heard about the Indian looting and sent a contingent of 200 soldiers under Colonel William Gregg to stop them. Instead, on August 14, Gregg ran into Baum's force at a flour mill about nine miles from Bennington. There were too few Americans to stop Baum, so they fired a single volley, destroyed a bridge, and retreated. Baum immediately sent off a dispatch to Burgoyne explaining that he had captured some supplies, and adding that he had found out that a much larger force of Americans was awaiting him at Bennington. However, Baum said that he did not intend to retreat.

On August 15, it rained heavily. Because Baum was outnumbered, he planned to take up a defensive position outside Bennington. On a hill along the Walloomsac River, Baum entrenched some of his men behind a breastwork of logs that they had built. A second contingent with several cannon was entrenched on another hill nearby. Baum himself took up a position on a road in the center. Across the Walloomsac River, Baum placed a third group, including his Indian warriors.

Stark sent out scouts to find out where the Germans had positioned themselves. He realized that they had probably spread their forces far too thin, so that no contingent could easily support another. Stark and Colonel Warner decided that since they outnumbered Baum almost three to one, they would try to strike him at three different places simultaneously. One contingent would hit him on the left flank, another on the right flank, and Stark would attack in the center. This would confuse Baum, and give his men no time to support each other's positions.

By noon on August 16, 1777, the skies began clearing. Stark's men moved into position through dense woods, trying to prevent the Germans from seeing them. A three-pronged attack depends on perfect timing. Each contingent must be in place and advance simultaneously to have the maximum impact. Stark's troops executed the plan perfectly. The battle began about 3:00 P.M. As Stark signaled his men to attack, he reportedly said: "There are your enemies, the Hessians and the Tories. We must beat them or tonight Molly Stark [my wife] sleeps a widow."

The struggle for the entrenched position on the hill was fierce. The American troops charged amid the smoke from their musket fire, but they were beaten back by the German defenders. However, the militia kept advancing, and finally swarmed over the German position. As one American soldier put it: "The day was very warm. They were in full dress & very heavy armed and we in our shirts and trousers. . . . Some were killed in their works. Many were killed and taken in going down the hill and others on the flat upon the river." Across the river, the Indians and Tories had met a similar fate; they were overcome after firing a single volley. However, Colonel Baum continued to hold his position with a contingent of German soldiers. Eventually, they ran out of ammunition. But still they kept fighting. Baum ordered his men to use their musket butts to club the enemy and charge them with bayonets. However, there were too many American

American soldiers beat back the German infantry at the Battle of Bennington, August 16, 1777.

militias. As the Germans retreated, Baum was hit by a bullet and fell to the ground. The Germans had seen enough and began to surrender.

Some of Stark's men now began to gather up the prisoners. Others were exhausted from the hard fought battle and stopped during the hot afternoon to rest and drink water. Still others started looting the German camp and stealing possessions from the German dead. While Stark's men were scattered across the battlefield, some of them spotted another army of German soldiers approaching from the west. General Burgoyne had sent out reinforcements under the command of Lieutenant Colonel Heinrich Breymann. His force included over 600 men as well as artillery. Breymann had marched slowly through the mud and rain from the main British position along the Hudson. By the time he had reached the battlefield, Baum was already defeated. But Breymann did not know it, and he ordered his men to advance against Stark's militia.

As Breymann recalled: "I noticed through the woods a considerable number of armed men . . . hastening towards an eminence on my left flank. I thereupon ordered [one] battalion . . . to move toward the height. . . . The engagement now commenced and lasted until near eight o'clock. The cannon were posted on a road where there was a log house. This we fired upon as it was occupied by the rebels. This drove them out and we then repulsed them on all sides and . . . notwithstanding they received reinforcements."

An American soldier recalls encountering the Hessian reinforcements: ". . . we met Breymann with 800 fresh troops and larger cannon which opened fire of grape shot. Some of the grape shot riddled a . . . fence near me, one struck a small white oak tree behind which I stood. Though it hit higher than my head I fled from the tree thinking it might be aimed at again." At first the Americans were pushed back by Breymann's troops. But Colonel Seth Warner arrived on the battlefield to take command of the scattered American forces. A fresh contingent also arrived from Vermont. "Fix bayonets! Charge!" Warner yelled. By this time, Breymann's troops had almost run out of ammunition. Stark had also rallied

Statue of Colonel Seth Warner, who took command on the battle-field at Bennington and helped defeat the German reinforcements led by Colonel Heinrich Breymann.

some of his troops who were fighting alongside Warner. It was too much for the Germans, who turned around and retreated from the battlefield. Gradually, they began running down the road with the Americans firing toward them from the flanks and the rear.

As the battlefield became dark, Breymann and most of his men escaped. He later wrote a letter to General Burgoyne, but did not mention the rout of his soldiers: "The troops did their duty, and I know of no one who doubts this fact. After our ammunition was all expended, and the artillery . . . ceased firing, nothing was more natural than to suppose that the enemy would be encouraged to renew his attack. . . . I retreated on the approach of darkness."

General Burgoyne, however, was sadly disappointed with Breymann's performance. But the British commander had only himself to blame for the outcome. In sending Baum, General Burgoyne had picked the wrong man. He should have sent a more experienced commander, at least one who understood English. As Baum saw the American militia advance on the day of the battle, he thought they were Tories. Therefore, Baum had given orders that his pickets should retreat and let the "Tories" advance. This only increased the surprise when the battle began and allowed the American troops to get closer to the German position and fire their muskets with greater accuracy.

In addition to sending out the wrong commander, Burgoyne was indecisive regarding the purpose of the mission. He sent too many men for a quick hit and run raid to obtain supplies. But he sent too few men to engage a substantial force of American troops. As a result, Baum's mission was almost doomed from the beginning.

The American army under General John Stark and Colonel Seth Warner had won an impressive victory at Bennington. With a loss of about 70 men, they had killed or captured more than 900 German soldiers. These soldiers were now unavailable to General Burgoyne for the rest of the campaign. Furthermore, the Americans had prevented Burgoyne from obtaining any supplies at

Bennington. He could not now risk sending out another force to find food and horses in Vermont. Instead, he would need to rely on his long supply line from Canada. Finally, the American victory probably discouraged most Tories from Vermont or New Hampshire from joining the British army.

What had begun for the British with a victory at Fort Ticonderoga was now turning to defeat. And more bad news for Burgoyne was about to follow from the Mohawk River valley.

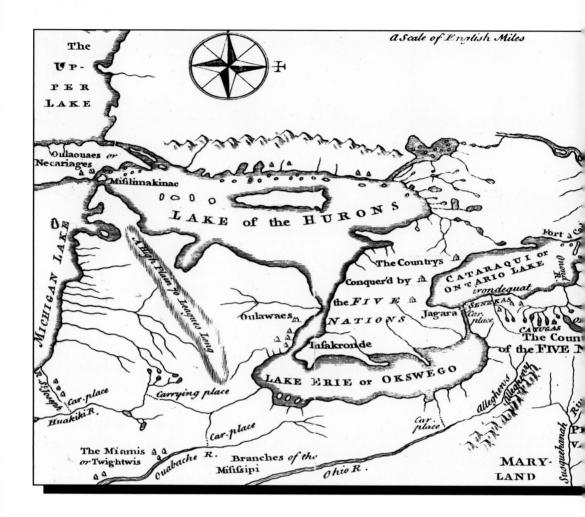

The Countrys
Conquer'd by
the FIVE NATIONS

CATARAQUI or ONTARIO LAKE

The Upper Lake

A Scale of English Miles

Oulaouaes or Necariages

Misilimakinac

LAKE of the HURONS

MICHIGAN LAKE

A High Plain 7 leagues long

Oulawaes

Insakronde

LAKE ERIE or OKSWEGO

Carrying place

Car-place

R. St Joseph

Car-place

Huakiki R.

The Miamis or Twightwis

Ouabache R.

Branches of the Misisipi

Ohio R.

Car-place

Jagara Car-place

SENEKAS

CAYUGAS

The Country of the FIVE N

Fort

Irondequat

Alleghens

Alleghery

Susquehanah Riv

MARY-LAND

Victory Along the Mohawk

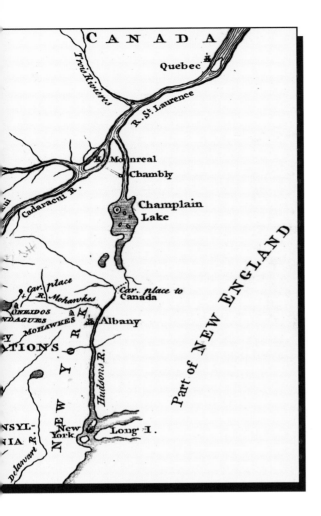

The lands of the six Iroquois nations stretched from the Hudson River across New York to Lake Ontario. The Six Nations had formidable warriors, and their allegiance was sought by both the British and American armies.

While Burgoyne was advancing southward, he had sent another army down from Canada to Lake Ontario, ordering it to advance along the Mohawk River Valley and link up with his main force. Along the way, this army was supposed to enlist the support of the powerful Iroquois nations and persuade them to rise up against the Americans who lived in the Mohawk Valley.

In 1777, the villages of the six Iroquois nations stretched from the Hudson River westward to Lake Ontario. Nearest the Hudson lay the lands of the Mohawks, followed by the Oneidas who lived along the Mohawk River, the Onondagas, the Cayugas, and the Senecas, while to the south lay the hunting grounds of the

Tuscoraras. The Iroquois formed a confederacy, which had originally been founded during the 16th century by a legendary Onondaga chief, Hiawatha. The Iroquois sachems met together at the capital of the confederacy in Onondaga, located in western New York. Here they debated important issues, such as whether the confederacy should declare war. Decisions had to be unanimous, or the Iroquois could not act together. However, in the absence of agreement, each tribe was free to act on its own.

Onondaga was a prosperous Indian capital lying on a river that, according to travelers, flowed through "a very beautiful and fertile" valley, while the town itself was filled with "a strange mixture of cabins interspersed with great patches of high grass, bushes and shrubs, some of peas, corn, and squashes." The Iroquois were not only successful farmers, but also aggressive traders and warriors. During the 17th century they had become the primary middlemen in the lucrative fur trade. Since beaver had mostly disappeared in the land of the Iroquois, there were no furs to trade for guns and other items which Dutch and British merchants sold at Albany. Therefore, the Iroquois waged a series of successful wars against tribes such as the Huron to replace them as middlemen. The Iroquois could then carry furs from the western Indians to Albany in return for trade goods to barter with the tribes. However, the Albany merchants often paid low prices for furs, and the Iroquois soon learned they could make a better deal if they traded with both the British and the French, playing one against the other. During the 18th century the Albany merchants were trying to get around the Iroquois by trading directly with the French in Montreal. This, of course, greatly angered the Six Nations.

Stepping into this tangled political situation in 1738 was a young Irishman named William Johnson. He set up a farm and a trading post along the Mohawk River and

Sir William Johnson, an English trader and colonial administrator, befriended the Iroquois and maintained their alliance with Great Britain.

quickly won a reputation for giving the Iroquois fair prices for their furs, far better than they received in Albany. Johnson also had a genuine interest in the Iroquois culture. He learned the Mohawk language, danced and sang with the Mohawks in their tribal celebrations, and was eventually adopted into the Mohawk tribe. They called him *Warraghiyagey*, "a man who undertakes great things."

Johnson's influence among the Iroquois was eventually recognized by the British authorities in Albany who named him Colonel of the Six Nations and their Allies in 1755. That same year, Johnson led the Iroquois to a victory against the French on Lake George. During the French and Indian War, he helped maintain Iroquois neutrality, and the Six Nations did not join the French when they won a string of victories against the British in 1756 and 1757. The Iroquois might have put at least 1,500 warriors in the field and decimated the Mohawk River valley. Finally when the tide turned in favor of Great Britain, many of the Iroquois agreed to go to war against France. After the war, Johnson continued to handle Indian affairs for the British government from his home at Johnson Hall on the banks of the Mohawk River. He had even married a Mohawk woman named Molly Brant, further strengthening his ties with the Iroquois.

Johnson died in 1774, and his position was taken over by his son, John Johnson, and nephew, Guy Johnson. Another influential leader among the Iroquois was Joseph Brant, the brother of Molly Brant. Joseph Brant had been educated at a school for Indians in Lebanon, Connecticut, fought along side William Johnson during the French and Indian War, traveled to England, and even had his portrait painted—a sign of wealth and prestige in those times. His role, along with the Johnsons, would become crucial during the Revolutionary War.

In 1775, as the war began, the Six Iroquois nations met in a large council to decide what role they should play. The Confederacy eventually decided to remain neutral. However, Brant believed that this decision was a tremendous mistake. He was afraid that if the Americans won the war, they would continue pushing westward and deny the Iroquois their ancestral homes. Under his influence, four of the Iroquois tribes—the

Mohawks, Onondagas, Cayugas, and Senecas—formed an alliance with Great Britain.

In the meantime, John Johnson was defending Johnson Hall where 700 of his soldiers had taken up a fortified position. Early in 1776, General Schuyler advanced with an army of 3,000 men to force Johnson out of the Mohawk Valley. Eventually, Johnson decided to surrender and agreed never again to make war against the American armies. Only a few months later, however, he left the valley and fled north to Canada. Here he raised a new army, called the Royal Greens because of the color of their uniforms, and prepared to return to New York.

In July 1777, an army commanded by Lt. Colonel Barry St. Leger left Canada for Lake Ontario and an invasion of the Mohawk Valley. St. Leger's force of about 900 men included the Royal Greens, commanded by John Johnson, a unit of Tories under the leadership of Colonel John Butler, as well as almost 1,000 Iroquois led by Joseph Brant. They were marching toward Fort Stanwix, an American stronghold on the Mohawk River near the Great Carrying Place. This was the area between Wood Creek and the Mohawk where travelers had to carry or transport their boats.

Fort Stanwix had been built during the French and Indian War. It was a logical defensive location for a fort because an invading French army would follow this route from Canada and pass over the Great Carrying Place to reach the Mohawk River. Built under the direction of General John Stanwix, the fort was constructed of logs and earth and included four large pointed bastions, one on each corner. After the war had ended, the fort was not kept in good condition because there seemed to be no need for it any longer. In April 1777, Colonel Peter Gansevoort arrived at the fort, and, along with his second in command,

Built during the French and Indian War, Fort Stanwix guarded the Mohawk River Valley against an invasion by the French from Canada. The American army used the fort to the same end under the command of Colonel Gansevoort in 1777.

Lieutenant Colonel Marinus Willet, they began to improve its condition to withstand an attack. By June, Native Americans had already begun to send out raiding parties in the Mohawk Valley in advance of the British invasion. Two

soldiers were attacked, tomahawked, and scalped about a mile from Fort Stanwix. In early July, a group of seven men were ambushed by Indians who killed one of them and took four prisoners. By the end of the month, St. Leger's army had reached Wood Creek. Here they were delayed by large trees that the Americans had cut to block their boats from moving along the water. On August 2, just before St. Leger arrived in front of Fort Stanwix, several boats filled with supplies as well as reinforcements of about 200 men reached the defenders at the fort, bringing their total force to about 750 soldiers.

"Next morning," Willet later wrote, "the enemy appeared in the edge of the woods about a mile below the fort, where they took post, in order to invest it." Then St. Leger sent an ultimatum to Gansevoort calling on him to surrender. In order to persuade him to accept the ultimatum, St. Leger ordered his troops and Native Americans to march in front of the fort. The Americans, however, were not intimidated and refused to hand over Fort Stanwix to the British.

Willett wrote that while his men were trying to put pieces of sod on the walls of the fort to make it higher, they were "much annoyed by a sharp fire of musketry from the Indians and . . . riflemen, as our men were obliged to be exposed on the works, [who] killed one man and wounded seven. The day after, the firing was not so heavy, and our men were under better cover; all the damage was one man killed by a rifle ball." On the evening of August 4, Willet reported that "the Indians were uncommonly noisy, they made most horrid yellings great part of the evening in the woods, hardly a mile from the fort. A few cannon shot were fired among them."

While the Americans were trying to maintain their position, a relief force was on its way to help the fort. General Nicholas Herkimer had gathered the force east of Fort Stanwix. The son of a German immigrant, Herkimer had become a successful farmer and trader, and held a prominent position among the many Germans who had settled in the Mohawk Valley. Once his men were assembled, Herkimer had asked for volunteers to bring messages to Fort Stanwix. In case one was caught by the enemy, he sent several with the same message; he asked the fort's defenders to fire three cannon and attack the English camp when the messengers arrived, distracting them as Herkimer's relief force approached the fort.

Herkimer waited with his 800-man army until he heard the cannon shots. But none came. The general and his officers discussed whether to advance even without the signal and finally decided to move ahead. In the meantime, St. Leger had heard about the approach of the relief force and sent out some of his men to set a trap for it. Near the Oriskany village, the road to Fort Stanwix ran through a deep ravine. On August 6, 1777, St. Leger sent the Royal Greens led by Colonel Butler and the Iroquois under Joseph Brant to hide in the woods surrounding the ravine. As Herkimer and his men advanced along it, Brant and Butler planned to attack.

Apparently, Herkimer failed to send out any flankers who might have seen the enemy hidden in the woods, and his men walked directly into the trap. Firing began just as the head of Herkimer's column of troops were reaching the end of the ravine. Some of his troops were immediately shot and killed before they could even fire. Others tried to fire at the Indians, but as the American militiamen reloaded, Indian warriors would charge and tomahawk them. During the opening of the battle, Herkimer himself had his horse shot out from under him and his leg was wounded. His men wanted him to leave the battlefield, but he ordered them to carry him to a nearby tree. There he sat, smoking his pipe and directing the battle.

Joseph Brant was an influential Iroquois leader. Iroquois led by
Brant ambushed a group of American militia, led by General
Nicholas Herkimer, at the Battle of Oriskany.

Gradually, the American militia gained a position on
a hill overlooking the ravine and defended it against their
attackers. As the battle raged, the skies darkened and a
heavy rain began. Since the rain dampened the powder
that the soldiers put in their rifles to fire musket balls, the

shooting suddenly stopped. Once the rain was over, the fighting resumed. By this time, Herkimer had told his men that they should fight in pairs against the Indians. As one soldier fired and then stopped to reload, the other could defend him by firing against an attacking warrior.

More and more Native Americans were now being hit, and Brant's warriors were beginning to lose their initial advantage in the battle. Suddenly, cannon shots were heard from the direction of Fort Stanwix. These shots were followed by rifle fire as the defenders advanced from the fort. Under the direction of Colonel Willett, about 250 men attacked the British camp, which was lightly defended. They captured a large quantity of supplies and returned to the fort without any casualties.

At Oriskany the Indians began to retreat from the battlefield with cries of *"Oonah! Oonah!"* After hearing the cannon fire from Fort Stanwix, they had decided to return there. Butler's Greens, who were now outnumbered by the Americans, also retreated. The Battle of Oriskany, which had lasted most of the day, had been a draw. Although the Greens and the Iroquois had withdrawn from the battlefield, they had stopped the relief force from reaching Fort Stanwix. The American militia had lost several hundred men who were killed or wounded in a very bloody battle and retreated eastward. General Herkimer died after his leg was amputated a few days after the battle.

St. Leger continued his siege of Fort Stanwix. Once again, he called on the Americans to surrender, but they refused even after being told that General Herkimer had been defeated at Oriskany. Instead, Colonel Willett was given a mission to sneak through the enemy lines and try to reach General Schuyler's headquarters near Albany where he might be able to gather another relief force. Schuyler had already heard that the British were besieging

As the tide of the Battle of Oriskany turned, many of the Iroquois warriors led by Brant were killed or wounded. They returned to Fort Stanwix, where they prevented reinforcements from reaching the Americans.

Fort Stanwix and wanted to send an army to help its defenders. But some of his officers opposed this decision, fearing that it might weaken the main army that was opposing Burgoyne. According to one historian, Schuyler

Barry St. Leger

Barry St. Leger was born in England in 1737. After attending college at Cambridge University, St. Leger joined the British Army in 1756. At this time, the Seven Years War was breaking out in Europe. England and its ally, King Frederick the Great of Prussia, were fighting against France and Austria. St. Leger became an officer in an infantry regiment and sailed to North America.

Over the next three years, St. Leger participated in several of the most important campaigns during the French and Indian War. In 1757, he served under General James Abercrombie who was trying to defend the New York frontier against the French. However, Abercrombie's efforts were unsuccessful, and French General Louis Montcalm captured Fort William Henry. This important British outpost guarded the base of Lake George in New York. The following year, St. Leger was sent north where he fought during the siege of Louisbourg. Located on Cape Breton Island, near Nova Scotia, Louisburg was a large French citadel which guarded the St. Lawrence River. Under the leadership of General Jeffrey Amherst and General James Wolfe, the British laid siege to the massive fortress and captured it in July, 1758. The following year, St. Leger joined Wolfe's army at the successful siege of Quebec, and in 1760 helped capture the French citadel at Montreal.

During the American Revolution, St. Leger, now a Lieutenant Colonel, was selected to capture Fort Stanwix. Although this expedition failed, he continued to participate in the war. From his base at Montreal, St. Leger led a force of British rangers who harassed the American troops. In 1781, he was sent on an expedition to capture General Philip Schuyler. However, this mission failed. After the war, St. Leger returned to Canada. He died in 1789.

was so angry that he bit the stem of his clay pipe in half. "Gentlemen," he said, "I shall take the responsibility upon myself. Fort Stanwix and the Mohawk Valley shall be saved! Where is the [general] who will command the relief?"

That general was Benedict Arnold, who volunteered to lead a relief column to Fort Stanwix. With a force of approximately 1,000 troops, he moved swiftly down the valley. Although Arnold had been told that St. Leger's outnumbered his army, he continued to advance. In addition, he tried to trick St. Leger into believing that the American army was far bigger than it really was. Arnold's men had captured a Tory named Hon Yost Schuyler and sentenced him to hang for recruiting soldiers to help the British. Schuyler often acted in a crazy way, appearing to be mentally ill. Among the Indians, the mentally ill were thought to have great wisdom given to them by God. Schuyler made General Arnold an offer: If the general agreed to free him, he would go to St. Leger's camp and spread the word among the Indians, some of whom he may have known, that a large army was approaching.

Hon Yost Schuyler traveled westward and entered the British siege lines. He claimed to have barely escaped from the Americans with his life and told the Indians that Arnold was approaching with several thousand troops. This was a much greater force than the Indians could withstand, and they immediately began to leave the British camp. Without the Indians, St. Leger had too few men to continue the siege and retreated westward. The trick had worked, and before Arnold reached Fort Stanwix on August 24, the siege had ended.

Suddenly, Burgoyne had lost another part of his army. The British withdrawal also meant that the Native Americans and Tories in the Mohawk Valley who might have joined Burgoyne decided instead to sit out the rest of the campaign. The standoff at the Battle of Oriskany, combined with American victories at Fort Stanwix and the Battle of Bennington, had greatly reduced the strength of Burgoyne's invasion. Gradually, the odds of a British victory were growing worse and worse.

In August 1777, General Horatio Gates took command of the American army opposing the British invasion of the Hudson Valley. The Continental Congress had become frustrated with General Schuyler's constant defeats and retreats from the British army.

The Battle of Freeman's Farm

While the Mohawk Valley campaign was still underway, General Philip Schuyler was replaced as commander of the American army in northern New York. The Continental Congress had lost faith in Schuyler following the defeat at Fort Ticonderoga, coupled with his constant retreats from the advancing British army. In addition, the New England militia did not like Schuyler because of his Dutch ancestry, and they resented the fact that he was a wealthy landowner while they were small farmers and merchants. The New Englanders also found Schuyler arrogant and aloof, accusing him of spending far more time living at his mansion in upstate New York rather than remaining with them and sharing the harsh life in the army camp.

Whatever his faults may have been, General Schuyler had provided a valuable service to the army he commanded. In the face of Burgoyne's superior forces, Schuyler had little choice but to retreat because the American army was much too weak to confront the British in a decisive battle. In the meantime, he had stretched Burgoyne's supply line almost to the breaking point, while keeping the American army together and its soldiers from panicking and deserting. Schuyler had also engineered the victory at Fort Stanwix and the failure of St. Leger's expedition in the Mohawk Valley. In short, he had bought time for the American army to grow stronger so it could defeat the British.

Schuyler was replaced by Horatio Gates, a veteran of the French and Indian War and a member of General Washington's staff. General Gates inherited an army whose morale was low because of its numerous retreats, but as one of his biographers put it: "Gates had an electrifying effect upon the Northern army for a number of reasons. For one thing, he held a high opinion of the New England troops that formed the backbone of the army. Yankee soldiers responded by showing a great affection for this little gray-haired general who came to be known as 'the darling of the New Englanders.' Gates also earned the respect of his men by sharing with them the rigors of camp life."

As a result of Gates's arrival in August 1777, more militia began to join the army. Many joined because they were also outraged at the murder of Jane McCrea by several of Burgoyne's Indian allies. Following the victories at Bennington and Fort Stanwix, many Americans began to sense that the tide was turning in the North. By the beginning of September, the army had reached 7,000 soldiers. General Arnold had returned with his men from the Mohawk Valley. In addition, General Washington had sent more than 300 riflemen north under the leadership of one of the army's most successful field commanders, Daniel Morgan.

Morgan had known Washington since the 1750s when they fought together in the French and Indian War. During the war he had been disciplined by a British officer and given 500 lashes across his back. Morgan never forgot the beating or forgave the British. He joined the American army in 1775 after war broke out, and fought alongside Benedict Arnold at the battle of Quebec. Morgan's riflemen were crack shots and hardened veterans who could play a key role in any major battle.

Soon after Morgan's arrival, the American army advanced northward. This, in itself, heartened the soldiers who had known nothing but retreat. General Gates had decided to take up a position on some bluffs that arose along the western bank of the Hudson River. They were called Bemis Heights in honor of a man named Jotham Bemis who owned a nearby tavern. Thaddeus Kosciuszko, the polish engineer who served with the army, had laid out a series of defensive works along Bemis Heights. Following his plan, the American soldiers constructed a large "U" shaped breastwork made of logs and dirt, and hauled up cannon to put at several points along the defensive structure. To protect the road that ran beside the river, the American soldiers dug a trench and put cannon behind it as well as a redoubt (protective barrier) with more cannon another mile up the road. By September 15, the army was completely ready for battle.

Although General Gates may have enjoyed a warm relationship with the New England militia, he did not believe they could stand up to the British regulars on an open battlefield. Gates thought the best chance of the army's success was a defensive position behind strong breast works. He was prepared to let the British army try to batter itself in a frontal attack against the Americans. Gates knew that

General Thaddeus Kosciuszko, a Polish engineer, designed defensive works for the American army along Bemis Heights near the Hudson River.

while his army was getting stronger, the British army was weakening. He reasoned that Burgoyne would have to force a battle because it was the only way he could reach Albany before winter set in.

The British general saw things about the same way that Gates had seen them. As Burgoyne marched down the east side of the Hudson River, he was faced with a choice. He

The Polish Engineer

Engineer Thaddeus Kosciuszko was born in Poland in 1746. He attended military school in Warsaw, Poland, then traveled to France. There he was trained in artillery and military engineering. Kosciuszko believed strongly in political freedom, so he volunteered his services to the American army after the outbreak of the Revolutionary War. He was one of many European soldiers who voluntarily helped the American army. Among the others was the Marquis de Lafayette of France and the Prussian General Frederich von Steuben.

During 1776, Kosciuszko helped to build up the defenses protecting Philadelphia, the capital of the new republic. The following year, he was sent north to assist General Horatio Gates in fortifying the American position at Bemis Heights. After the victory at Saratoga, Kosciuszko spent two years, 1778-1780, strengthening the fortifications at the American stronghold of West Point on the Hudson River. Kosciuszko later served as a cavalry leader as well as an engineer with the American army in the South during 1781.

After the American Revolution, Kosciuszko went home to Poland. During the 1790s, he defended his country against an invasion by the Russians. However, the Russian army was victorious, and Kosciuszko went to France. He later returned to Poland to continue fighting against the Russian invaders. Kosciuszko was captured, imprisoned, and later released. In 1797, he came back to the United States, where he was welcomed as a hero. Although he was given some land by the U.S. government, Kosciuszko decided that he did not want to settle in North America. Instead, he returned to Europe. Kosciuszko spent the rest of his life trying to convince the great nations of Europe to support Polish independence. However, he was unsuccessful in getting their help. He died in 1817 in Switzerland.

could remain on that side and try to bypass Gates's position. However, further south, where the river was much wider, Burgoyne would have to cross to the western side to attack Albany, which was located on that bank of the river. Or

Burgoyne could cross the Hudson north of Bemis Heights where the river was much narrower and risk everything on a single battle against the Americans.

As Gates's army was entrenching at Bemis Heights, Burgoyne built a bridge of boats across the Hudson River and his army crossed over to the western side, a few miles north of the American position. Burgoyne realized that he needed to concentrate all his troops and supplies for the coming battle against the American army. Therefore, he had ordered that everything be removed from Fort Edward and Fort Anne and brought southward. Although there were still troops at Fort Ticonderoga, the garrison there was reduced and many of the soldiers marched south to join Burgoyne. The British general had now cut his communications with Canada in order to make a final bold thrust southward. As he wrote to the British government in London: "The moment is a decisive one."

Burgoyne had no time to lose. His army had been reduced to about 6,000 soldiers, less than the Americans. He had enough supplies for about four weeks, but only because his men were forced to get along on reduced rations. Some of his soldiers were not satisfied with the amount of rations they received and decided to go on a foraging expedition to local farms. However, American riflemen ambushed the foraging soldiers, killing and wounded some of them.

Burgoyne's army took up a position at Saratoga on the west bank of the Hudson River and began to move toward the Americans. Since most of the Indians had deserted following the defeats in the Mohawk Valley, Burgoyne was not certain exactly where the Americans were located, but he sensed that Bemis Heights was their likely position. On the morning of September 19, 1777, the British army advanced to battle. General Simon Fraser, commanding the right, had been ordered by Burgoyne to occupy a hill to the west of Bemis Heights from which the British might bombard the American position. Burgoyne hoped to use the same tactic he had successfully employed at Ticonderoga several months. Commanding the British center was General James Hamilton, while Baron von Riedesel marched with his German troops along the river road on the British left flank. The British advanced to a steep ravine, which they crossed, and took up a position at one end of a large field that had been cleared from the thick woods, covering most of the area. The field had been owned by John Freeman and was called Freeman's Farm.

Although General Gates was aware that the British were advancing, he was content to keep his men inside their defensive position on Bemis Heights. However, Benedict Arnold believed that this tactic was a grave mistake. Arnold was afraid that a British flanking movement might occupy the hill to the west of Bemis Heights. He also feared that if the Americans could not hold the breastworks on the Heights there was nowhere for them to retreat and they might flee headlong down the road to Albany. Arnold strongly urged Gates to send out some of his soldiers to find out exactly where the British were headed. As one historian wrote: "Arnold persisted in his appeals. Gates, who seemed almost paralyzed by indecisiveness, finally relented, but probably only to stop Arnold from pestering him."

Gates sent out Daniel Morgan and his riflemen along with Colonel Henry Dearborn's light infantry. They arrived at one end of Freeman's Farm early in the afternoon, just as British advance pickets had reached the other side. Morgan's men took cover and launched a deadly fire at the British, hitting many of their officers. As the British began to retreat, the riflemen ran forward believing that the enemy's entire line was retreating. They met with a terrible surprise. One American officer recalled that "having forced the picket, they had closed with the British line, had been instantly routed, and from the suddenness of the shock and

Daniel Morgan led a contingent of experienced riflemen at the battles of Freeman's Farm and Bemis Heights.

the nature of the ground, were broken and scattered in all directions. . . . I then turned about to regain the camp and report . . . when my ears were saluted by an uncommon noise which I approached and perceived Colonel Morgan, attended by two men only, who with a *turkey call* was collecting his dispersed troops."

After his men had been hurled back by British reinforcements, Morgan tried desperately to reestablish his
position. General Gates, who remained back at headquarters, was told what was happening to Morgan and
immediately sent reinforcements to support him.
Historians have debated where Benedict Arnold was
located at this moment of the battle. But as least some of
the American soldiers saw him in the thick of the fighting, urging the Continentals to hold their ground
against the British. A fierce battle now raged around
Freeman's Farm, claiming the lives of many men on
each side. General Arnold saw an opening between the
British right wing and the center. He tried to drive his
troops through the opening so they could separate the
British army into two pieces and defeat each one of them
separately. As one soldier recalled: "Riding in front of
the line, his eyes flashing, pointing with his sword to the
advancing foe, with a voice that rung clear as a trumpet,
[he] called upon the men to follow him . . . and . . . he
hurled them like a tornado on the British line . . . nothing
could exceed the bravery of Arnold on this day." The
battle lines swayed back and forth as both sides fought
for control of the British artillery. At one point, the
Americans had driven back the British and taken
possession of the cannon, only to be driven back themselves. The battle continued throughout the afternoon.
But General Arnold was convinced that with a few more
men he could win an American victory. He begged
Gates to send him additional men, and the commanding
officer finally but reluctantly agreed. However, they
were not given sufficient instructions about which part
of the battlefield to reinforce and ended up going to the
wrong place.

Meanwhile, Burgoyne, who was commanding the
British forces from the center of the battlefield, realized that

his army needed immediate reinforcements. He sent a message to General von Riedesel on the river road ordering him to send some of his troops toward Freeman's Farm and hit the Americans in the right flank. Since Gates had neglected to send out any troops to advance against von Riedesel, he was free to march to the aid of Burgoyne. Von Riedesel struck the American right and pushed it backward. By this time it was already nightfall, and both sides withdrew and stopped the fighting. The Battle of Freeman's Farm was over. As one British officer put it: "This crash of cannon and musketry never ceased till darkness parted us, when they retired to their camp, leaving us masters of the field; but it was a dear bought victory."

The British had technically won the battle but at a huge cost—they suffered over 500 casualties, almost 10 percent of the entire army. That night, as the British remained at their positions, they "heard the groans of our wounded and dying at a small distance, yet could not assist them till morning, not knowing the position of the enemy, and expecting the action would be renewed at daybreak." General Burgoyne hoped to continue the battle on the morning of September 20. However, his subordinate officers convinced him that the army was not strong enough to keep fighting. Perhaps another attack by the British might have been enough to disorganize the Americans and force a retreat southward. But Burgoyne would never find out.

In the meantime, General Gates kept the bulk of his army on Bemis Heights. He had been afraid to make a major commitment of his men to the battle at Freeman's Farm, as Arnold had wanted. Instead, Gates reasoned, time was on his side and if he waited the British army would grow gradually weaker and be forced to destroy itself against his defensive works. As a result, some historians believe that Gates lost an opportunity to defeat Burgoyne at Freeman's Farm. Had the American general put more men

German soldiers under Baron von Riedesel stopped the American advance at the Battle of Freeman's Farm and probably saved General Burgoyne's army from defeat.

in the center of the field, as Arnold had asked, and sent a strong detachment along the river road so General von Riedesel could not have reinforced Burgoyne's center, the rebel army might have won a tremendous victory.

But Gates resented Arnold's interference, just as Arnold resented Gates's refusal to act more decisively. When Gates

General Horatio Gates decided not to commit the majority of his troops to the Battle of Freeman's Farm, and may have lost an opportunity to decisively defeat the British.

sent a report of the battle to the Continental Congress, he never mentioned Arnold's role in the victory. General Arnold was furious. While these disagreements raged in the American army, Burgoyne entrenched his army near Freeman's Farm on September 21. General Burgoyne had decided to wait where he was, because he had received a message from General Henry Clinton, commanding the

British troops in New York City. The message read in part: "You know my good will. . . . If you think 2000 men can assist you effectually, I will make a push . . . in about ten days."

General Clinton planned a small diversionary expedition that might draw off some of Gates's troops. Clinton proposed to attack Forts Montgomery and Clinton on the west bank of the Hudson River, south of Albany. This was the first good news Burgoyne had received in weeks. As he wrote to Clinton: "An attack or the menace of an attack, . . . must be of great use, as it will draw away part of this force and I will follow them close. Do it my friend directly." Burgoyne was hoping for any of kind of help. Otherwise he might be trapped where he was. Already, an American raiding party had attacked Mt. Defiance near Fort Ticonderoga, taken a number of British soldiers prisoner, and freed some captured rebel troops. This showed Burgoyne that his line of retreat to Canada could not be protected.

Burgoyne had informed Clinton that his food supplies would "not last him over a month" and hoped that Clinton would advance to Albany and meet Burgoyne there. But General Clinton had no plans to do anything but create a diversion. Clinton left New York and advanced up the Hudson. He landed his troops on the east side of the river to confuse American troops stationed nearby of his real plans. Then, under cover of a dense fog, Clinton recrossed the river and advanced rapidly against the American forts. The British attacked them in the rear, and after heavy fire from the American garrison, finally overwhelmed them and captured both Fort Clinton and Fort Montgomery. On October 8th, he wrote Burgoyne: "I sincerely hope this little success of ours may facilitate your operations. . . . I heartily wish you success." Clinton then retreated to New York City, leaving General Burgoyne and his troops on their own.

The British grenadier guards held the left flank of General Burgoyne's line at the Battle of Bemis Heights, October 7, 1777.

Victory at Bemis Heights

During the last week of September, the American and British armies faced each other from their entrenched positions. General Gates had ordered that the hill west of Bemis Heights be fortified. Meanwhile, General Burgoyne built several small forts along his line north of Freeman's Farm. One fort guarded the left flank near the Hudson River, another anchored the right flank, and a large fort was built in the rear of the line to protect it if the Americans tried to attack from that direction.

Time seemed on the side of the Americans. As more militia joined the army, there were approximately 11,000 soldiers serving. Burgoyne's force, on the other hand, was suffering desertions. General von Riedesel reported that the Americans were sending special agents to the British camp "who endeavored to induce the soldiers . . . to desert; and it being already known that the Americans treated their prisoners very kindly, and that they were not as strict in their discipline as the Europeans, the agents here and there found a willing ear." Since food was in short supply in the British army and far more plentiful on the American side, English and German deserters were glad to change sides.

Perhaps some of the soldiers also realized that the chances of English victory were growing slimmer and slimmer. Late in September, the army received word of the successful American attack on Mt. Defiance near Fort Ticonderoga, which effectively cut off any retreat northward. During the night, the American sentries also kept up a steady pressure against the British position near Freeman's Farm. As one British officer, Captain Thomas Anburey, wrote: " . . . the armies being so near . . . not a night passes but there is firing and continual attacks upon the advanced pickets especially those of the Germans. It seems to be the plan of the enemy to harass us by constant attacks, which they are enabled to do without fatiguing their army, from the great superiority of their numbers."

While the British tried to deal with the enemy confronting them, inside the Americans lines there was a serious internal conflict between Horatio Gates and Benedict Arnold who had disagreed about the way the Battle of Freeman's Farm had been handled. After Gates submitted his report to Congress, and never mentioned Arnold's role in the victory, Arnold had become even angrier with his commander. The two generals engaged in a heated argument, which ended with Gates replacing Arnold as one of his commanding officers. Arnold withdrew to his headquarters, highly offended at how he had been treated. Although he remained in camp, he planned to take no part in any upcoming battles.

While this conflict was occurring inside the American camp, the British commanders were planning one more attempt to achieve a military breakthrough and march to Albany. On October 4, General Burgoyne met with his commanding officers and proposed a plan for a massive assault against the left wing of the American army. General von Riedesel disagreed, pointing out that they had very little information about the American position so an attack could easily fail. Von Riedesel, instead, urged Burgoyne to retreat across the Hudson River and try to reestablish communications with Canada. General Fraser supported von Riedesel's position. Burgoyne, however, refused to consider retreating. Instead he proposed that a force of about 1,500 men be sent out on a reconnaissance mission to get more information about the American left wing. If they discovered that this position could be successfully attacked, then reinforcements might be sent in immediately. This was similar to the plan that had taken Colonel Baum to Bennington with too many men for a reconnaissance but not enough to win a battle. In trying to hedge, Burgoyne once more committed a terrible mistake.

On the morning of October 7, 1777, Burgoyne's troops advanced to a position about half way between Freeman's Farm and Bemis Heights. General Fraser and the Earl of Balcarres held the right, General von Riedesel the center, and on the left were the British grenadiers—the finest troops in the army. The English and Germans stopped on a slight hill, with woods on both sides and a wheat field in front. Foragers went into the field to cut the wheat, while some officers climbed on top of the roof of a cabin to catch sight of the American lines with telescopes. The American pickets had spotted the British advance, and Major James

Wilkinson took the information back to General Gates. Wilkinson began:

> "They are foraging, and endeavoring to reconnoiter your left and I think, sir, they offer you battle."

> "What is the nature of the ground, and what your opinion?"

> "Their front is open, and their flanks rest on woods, under cover of which they may be attacked; their right is skirted by a lofty height. I would indulge them."

> "Well, then, order on Morgan to begin the game."

Gates ordered Daniel Morgan on a flanking movement to swing way around the British right. A force of militia and Continentals under the command of General Enoch Poor would assault the enemy left, while a third unit commanded by Colonel Ebenezer Learned would attack the center. This force far outnumbered the 1,500 men sent out by Burgoyne. As Poor's men reached the British position, heavy rounds of grape shot from the artillery struck them. Much of the grape shot flew high and hit the leaves of the trees through which Poor's men had advanced without being seen. Most of the grape shot went high over their heads. They held their fire, and as the British charged, the American troops unleashed a blistering volley that sent the grenadiers reeling backward. The Americans captured their artillery pieces. Meanwhile, Learned sent his men on a successful attack against the Germans in the center.

On the right flank, Daniel Morgan's men had worked their way to the rear of the British position. Morgan's soldiers were met with a hail of grape shot, but made a gallant charge, pushing back the enemy. By this time, news of the battle had reached General Gates at headquarters.

General Enoch Poor led a force of American soldiers that attacked the British left flank at the Battle of Bemis Heights.

According to one account, his immediate subordinates, including General Arnold who was apparently eager to participate in the battle, had joined him. Arnold said to Gates: "'Shall I go out and see what is the matter?' General Gates made no reply, but upon being pressed, said, 'I am afraid to trust you, Arnold.' To which Arnold answered,

Field Artillery

General Burgoyne brought artillery with his army during the Saratoga campaign. The British used this artillery during the battles at Freeman's Farm and Bemis Heights. Most of the artillery consisted of field cannon. These could fire solid balls at an advancing army or at the enemy's fortified positions. Field artillery was also used to fire grape shot and canister. Grape shot consisted of iron balls wrapped in canvas. After the grape shot was fired, the canvas would open up and the balls would fly out. These could kill or injure several of the enemy. Grape was also used against fortifications. Canister consisted of a case loaded with small lead balls. After firing, the balls would fly out of the canister. This was especially effective at wounding many soldiers.

In battle, each artillery piece was drawn into place by ropes pulled by a gun crew. Once a cannon was in position, the crew would aim the artillery. A bag of powder was then rammed down the barrel from the front of the gun. Then a cannon ball or can of canister or bag of grape was rammed down after it. Powder was also used to prime a vent hole at the rear of the cannon over the bag of powder. Then a match was put to the vent hole and the cannon fired. After firing, the barrel had to be cleaned with wet sheepskin. Otherwise, sparks left in the barrel might ignite a new charge of powder accidentally, blowing up the gun and killing the crew.

In addition to field cannon, the armies of the Revolutionary War also relied on other types of artillery. These included howitzers which could shoot a projectile on a high arc into the air at the enemy. Howitzers were used to lob shells over the wall, fort, or fortified position. In addition, the armies used mortars. These were similar to howitzers. They had short stubby barrels and could also shoot projectiles at a high arcing trajectory. Howitzers and mortars regularly used exploding shot against their targets.

'Pray let me go. I will be careful, and if our advance does not need support, I will promise not to commit you.'"

Before Gates could reply, General Arnold had left the room, borrowed a nearby horse, and headed for the battlefront. Arnold first reached General Poor's units.

After asking whose men they were and finding out that some of them had come from Connecticut, Arnold's home state, he said: "God bless you! Now, come on boys, if the day is long enough, we'll have them all in hell before night!" Almost immediately, Arnold launched an attack against the German troops, but they had been reinforced and beat back the assault.

In the meantime, General Fraser had been trying to rally his troops, riding across the lines encouraging his men to hold their positions. Arnold spotted him and said to Morgan: "That officer upon a grey horse . . . must be disposed of—direct the attention of some of the sharp-shooters amongst your riflemen to him." Morgan called on one of his riflemen and said: "That gallant officer is General Fraser. I admire him, but it is necessary that he should die, do your duty." The rifleman, named Tim Murphy, hoisted himself into a tree and fired at Fraser; the first shot missed. He fired again, but missed a second time. Once more the riflemen aimed his musket and squeezed the trigger. The third shot knocked Fraser off his horse. With General Fraser out of action, General Burgoyne, who was in the thick of the fighting, ordered the British line to retreat to the fortified position north of Freeman's Farm.

Here the battle might have ended. However, General Arnold still believed that the Americans could win a complete victory and he led his forces toward the British entrenchment. According to several observers, Arnold was "raging like a madman" as he drove his horse across the battlefield. He might have easily been shot by a British musket ball, but somehow he escaped injury. First, Arnold attacked near the center of the British line but was beaten back. He then galloped across the battle-field and led some of Colonel Learned's men against several cabins that the British had fortified on the right side of their line. The Americans easily overwhelmed the defenders and began to sweep in behind the fort that the British had constructed in their rear. At the same time another American unit in the front was attacking this fort. The German soldiers commanded by Lt. Colonel von Breymann fired back at the advancing Americans. Von Breymann, who was considered a tough disciplinarian, beat his soldiers with his sword to prevent them from leaving the fort in the face of an overwhelming enemy charge. Finally one of the German soldiers turned his musket on von Breymann and killed him. The Germans retreated, and the Americans took control of the fort.

As the Germans fell back, they saw General Arnold. One of them shot Arnold's horse, which fell, breaking the general's leg and putting him out of action. When asked where he had been wounded, Arnold pointed to his leg. "I wish it had been my heart," he said. Arnold believed that if the battle had continued for just a little longer, he might have won a complete victory and forced Burgoyne to surrender.

Darkness was already falling, and both sides decided to call off the fight. Called by some historians the Battle of Bemis Heights and by others the Second Battle of Freeman's Farm, it had been an American victory. General Gates's losses were only about 150 men, while the British had lost over 600; among them was General Fraser who died on the day after the battle. The despair on the British side was easy to see, although Burgoyne tried to claim that he had won the battle.

Historians disagree about who should be given credit for the American victory at Bemis Heights. Historian Rupert Furneux wrote: "Arnold's heroic intervention contributed nothing to the battle that had already been won by General Gates." Furneux believed that Gates had already sent out a force under Daniel Morgan that was far

General Benedict Arnold was wounded while leading his troops against the British during the American victory at the Battle of Bemis Heights.

superior to the 1,500 men under General Simon Fraser. The early action of Morgan, Poor, and Learned would have driven Burgoyne back to his fortified position regardless of what Arnold had done. As a result, Gates and Morgan assured the American victory at Bemis Heights.

Historian Richard Ketchum disagrees. "Unlike Burgoyne," he wrote, "who chose . . . to be out on the front

After the Battle of Bemis Heights, the British remained at their positions and buried General Simon Fraser, who had been shot and killed during the battle.

lines with his troops . . . Gates never moved from his head-quarters, two miles from the battlefield, too far removed even to see what was happening. . . . As it happened, his only contributions to the battle on this day were the order to Morgan to circle around the British right, and sending out additional detachments while the fighting went on. . . . Benedict Arnold had many faults . . . yet it is not too much to say that this climactic battle was won in part because of his extraordinary bravery, magnetism, and energy." George

Athan Billias, one of Arnold's biographers, agrees: "Perhaps more than any single officer he had been responsible for the decisive American success."

Because of Benedict Arnold's intrepid leadership on the battlefield, Bemis Heights had been a decisive American victory. Had Burgoyne been allowed to retreat to the safety of his entrenched position, following the successful attack by Morgan, Learned, and Poor, British losses would not have been so great. Arnold's assault on the British entrenched position and the capture of the fort that the Germans had defended made it clear that Burgoyne could no longer remain on the battlefield. Another day's battle would destroy his army. As the size of the American forces grew larger, and Burgoyne's numbers dwindled, there seemed no reasonable chance for him to capture Albany. The British invasion was now over.

The Turning Point

The British were defeated at the Battle of Bemis Heights, and were forced to pull back to the safety of the redoubt at Saratoga. Burgoyne's hope of a decisive victory over the American rebels was crushed by the retreat.

General John Burgoyne was deeply troubled. As he took stock of his army on the evening of October 7, 1777, he saw a group of tired, bedraggled, beaten men. The Americans had turned his right flank during the day's battle, and Burgoyne was forced to move his men backward to the safety of a large fort, or redoubt, to prevent them from being encircled. But this was only the beginning of his problems. He had to face the fact that his dream of winning a tremendous victory and perhaps ending the war had ended. Burgoyne was an aristocrat and a showman who loved the pomp and ceremony of the British army, considered the greatest fighting force in the world. He was also a fearless leader, who had been in the thick of the fighting at Freeman's Farm and Bemis Heights. The general's men were devoted to the man they called "Gentleman Johnny." Burgoyne, himself, believed that they had fought hard enough to achieve a victory; instead they had suffered two humiliating defeats. Now he would be forced to give the one command that he had never issued during the entire campaign: retreat. It was a bitter pill for Burgoyne to swallow, especially because he had hoped that by his victory over the American rebels and his capture of Albany to become the most famous soldier in England.

Still, on the morning of October 8, Burgoyne hesitated to start his army on the march. Time was of the essence. If he intended to lead his men northward along the Hudson and back to Fort Ticonderoga, the British had to hurry. Winter was approaching. Even more importantly, the American forces might move in behind him and cut off his retreat. But the British lingered in camp until the evening, before beginning to move. If the American army had attacked, it might have destroyed the enemy. General Arnold would have attacked, but he was lying in camp with a serious wound. Horatio Gates was no Arnold. He decided to allow his men to rest, giving Burgoyne the time he needed to escape.

About nine o'clock, the British army moved eastward to the heights of Saratoga. Burgoyne had fortified this position earlier in September as he advanced toward Albany. The following day, October 9, the British retreat continued. But it moved extremely slowly because of heavy rains that made the roads almost impossible to use. The retreat was made even more miserable because American snipers kept firing from the rear. At one point, the army came to a complete halt, too exhausted to continue. Finally, the retreat resumed later in the afternoon, and the army eventually reached Saratoga where the men dug into their positions along the Hudson River. "Our retreat," wrote one of Burgoyne's officers, "was made within musket-shot of the enemy, and, though greatly encumbered with baggage, without a single loss."

If Burgoyne intended to make a dash for Fort Ticonderoga, he was moving far too slowly. But he was delayed by the rain, and his men were tired. Perhaps he also hoped that General Clinton was still advancing northward. Burgoyne had not heard from Clinton, and could not know that his soldiers had captured Forts Clinton and Montgomery and were preparing to turn around and head back to New York City.

Once he reached Saratoga, Burgoyne strengthened his defenses. He put one detachment to the north of the heights to guard that approach if the Americans should try to flank his position. In addition, he set up artillery to fire across the Hudson, in case the rebels tried to fire on his position from the east. In addition, Burgoyne sent a detachment of men northward toward Fort Edward to hold open a British escape route.

In the meantime, General Gates ordered part of his army to advance against the British position at Saratoga on October 10. Gates's spies had mistakenly reported that the British army had already begun its retreat toward Fort Ticonderoga, leaving only a rear guard at Saratoga. On the morning of October 11, the Americans were about to begin their attack when they captured a British deserter. He told them that the entire British army was still at Saratoga. Just in time, the American commanders called off their attack, or they would have hit the center of the British line and suffered a serious defeat. Gates decided to wait and continue firing at the British position with his cannon. Although he outnumbered Burgoyne more than three to one, General Gates saw no reason to risk a frontal attack. Instead, he sent Daniel Morgan to a position just northwest of Saratoga. Meanwhile Gates's main army remained to the south; and across the Hudson River, he had posted another American force with heavy artillery so the British could not escape in that direction. However, there was still a route open to the north along the west bank of the river, and the British might still take that road to safety.

On the afternoon of October 12, General Burgoyne met with his commanding officers to discuss their options. As one historian explained: "They were asked for their views on five possible courses of action. First, to stand at Saratoga, hoping to repel an enemy attack, and trusting that something might turn up. Second, to launch an attack. Third, to retreat, taking the guns with them, which would mean having to repair bridges en route. Fourth, to withdraw by night, abandoning guns and baggage. Fifth, to take advantage of Gates's extended left, slip past him, and march rapidly on Albany."

Burgoyne's officers believed that the only effective option was number four—withdrawing by night without their guns or baggage. This would enable the army to move quickly northward under cover of darkness. Trying to withstand another attack or continue the advance would only lead to disaster. However, the option was closed down almost immediately when a report came that the New Hampshire militia under the command of General John Stark had positioned themselves across the northward route along the west side of the Hudson River. For the British, the situation was hourly growing more desperate. As one soldier recalled: "Numerous parties of American militia . . . swarmed around the little . . . army like birds of prey. Roaring of cannon and whistling of bullets from their rifle pieces were heard constantly day and night."

Baron von Riedesel summed up the situation this way: "There was no place of safety for the baggage; and the ground was covered with dead horses that had either been killed by the enemy's bullets or by exhaustion. . . . Even for the wounded, no spot could be found which could afford them a safe shelter—not even, indeed, for so long a time as might suffice a surgeon to bind up their ghastly wounds."

On October 13, Burgoyne met with his commanders once again. At this meeting, they considered a sixth option: surrender. It seemed the only thing left for the army to do. The following day, Burgoyne sent Lieutenant Colonel Robert Kingston to General Gates. Kingston carried a message from Burgoyne saying that he was prepared to consider ending the conflict between the two armies if the Americans would give him honorable terms. Gates, however, demanded that Burgoyne agree to an unconditional surrender, which meant that all his troops would become prisoners of war. These were not the honorable terms that Burgoyne had in mind. Instead, he proposed that his men would put down their arms and march out of camp with safe passage being guaranteed back to England on condition of "not serving again in North America during the present contest."

General Gates agreed to these terms. He was eager to bring an end to the conflict because American spies had reported that the British were again moving up the Hudson. Although General Clinton had returned to New York, he had sent a small force northward. Burgoyne had received the same news regarding British troops from a Tory. Now he hesitated to accept Gates's terms of surrender. Perhaps there was still a chance the British army might be saved. But even Burgoyne realized that it was only a slim chance. His commanders told him that the honorable thing to do was to sign the surrender agreement since Gates had agreed to all the terms for which Burgoyne had asked.

On October 16, 1777, General Burgoyne signed the terms of surrender.

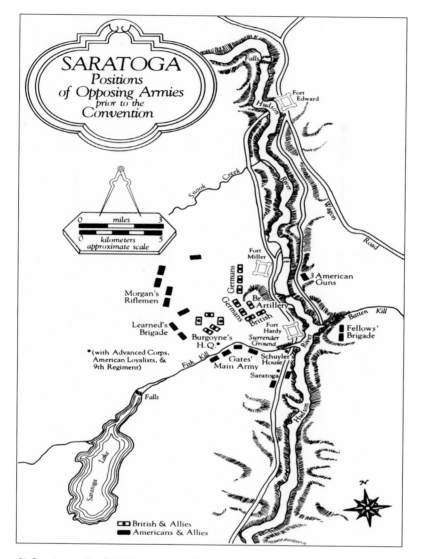

At Saratoga, the British were greatly outnumbered by the Americans, and had no possible avenue of escape. The victory at Saratoga convinced the French to form an alliance with the Americans and declare war on the British.

The following morning, the sound of fifes and drums drifted through the woodlands around Saratoga. After stacking their arms, the British and German soldiers marched out of camp toward the American lines. Ahead of the defeated army rode General John Burgoyne, resplendent in a bright scarlet coat and the insignias of a commanding general in the British army. He was followed by his aides and subordinate officers. Riding toward him, completely alone, was General Horatio Gates, much smaller than Burgoyne, wearing a simple faded blue coat. As the two generals approached each other, Burgoyne said: "The fortune of war, General Gates, has made me your prisoner." Gates answered him, very courteously, "I shall ever be ready to testify that it has not been through any fault of your Excellency." Burgoyne removed his sword and handed it to Gates, as the symbol of surrender. General Gates held it momentarily, and then gave it back to Burgoyne.

As the British troops marched into the American camp, one officer seemed surprised to discover that he and his men had been beaten by such an unusual army. He recalled: "They [the Americans] stood like soldiers, erect with a military bearing, so still that we were greatly amazed. . . . Not one of them was properly uniformed but each man had on the clothes in which he goes to the field, the church or to the tavern. . . . The officers wore very few uniforms and those they did wear were of their own invention." But the British were also amazed at how disciplined the American soldiers were as they stood completely silent and at attention. Some of the men were quite young, others were much older, in their fifties and sixties. Another British officer recalled that the American soldiers treated his men with the utmost honor. "They behaved with the greatest decency and propriety, not even a Smile appearing in any of their Countenances, which circumstance I really believe would not have happened had the case been reversed."

These soldiers had never before suffered such a defeat at the hands of the American army. In a letter to the Continental Congress, following the victory at Bemis

Burgoyne After Saratoga

After his surrender at Saratoga, General John Burgoyne returned to England. Many people there did not welcome him home. In fact, he was blamed for the defeat of the British army at the hands of the Americans. However, Burgoyne believed that he was not at fault for the British loss. Instead, he said that General William Howe was responsible. Howe, according to Burgoyne, should have brought his army north and caught the American army in a trap. However, Howe chose to attack Philadelphia. Burgoyne also blamed General Henry Clinton for not helping him. According to Burgoyne, his army might have been able to escape defeat at Saratoga if General Clinton had attacked Albany. However, Clinton returned to New York after only capturing two American forts on the Hudson River.

General Burgoyne never came back to America. For a short time, 1782-1783, he was appointed commander-in-chief of British forces in Ireland. But Burgoyne's real talents lay in the theater. In 1780, for example, he wrote part of an opera. Then, in 1786, Burgoyne published a play, titled "The Heiress." For an entire year, this play was the hit of the British stage. It was also performed on the European continent. General Burgoyne had finally found the fame that had escaped him as a military leader during the American Revolution.

General Burgoyne died on June 4, 1792. However, one of his sons made a name for himself in the British army. John Fox Burgoyne was an engineer who accompanied the British troops who invaded New Orleans during the War of 1812. Burgoyne participated in the Battle of New Orleans, which was fought in 1815. At that battle, General Andrew Jackson soundly beat the British army. Once again, a Burgoyne had been present at a major British defeat by an American army.

Heights, General Gates had lavishly praised the courage of his soldiers in battle. He had even singled out General Arnold for his role in the victory. Not only had the north been saved, the British also abandoned Fort Ticonderoga and retreated to Canada. The surrender at Saratoga came at

General John Burgoyne surrendered his army to General Horatio Gates at Saratoga, October 17, 1777.

an especially important moment for the American armies. Southward, in Pennsylvania, General Howe had defeated General Washington at the Battle of Brandywine Creek in September and captured the American capital at Philadelphia. The Continental Congress had moved to York, Pennsylvania. In an effort to defeat Howe, General Washington had attacked the British at Germantown, outside of Philadelphia. But after an initial success, the American troops had lost another battle.

Instead of Burgoyne becoming the most famous

commander in England, that honor went to General Howe. On October 20, General Burgoyne wrote a letter to Lord George Germain in London trying to explain the reasons for the surrender. As Burgoyne put it: "The British have persevered in a strenuous and bloody progress. . . . But as it was, will it be said, my Lord, that in the exhausted situation described, and in the jaws of famine, and invested by quadruple numbers, a treaty which saves the army to the state, for the next campaign, was not more than could have been expected? *I call it saving the army.*"

News of Gates's victory and Washington's defeats traveled quickly throughout America. It was December before the information finally reached France, carried by ship from the United States to Europe. The Continental Congress had sent three envoys to France: Benjamin Franklin, Silas Deane, and Arthur Lee. These men were trying to convince the French to join the war on the side of the American armies. During the early days of the Revolutionary War, France had sent the Americans some money and war supplies to carry on the conflict. But this was all the support that the French had given. While France had hoped to avenge its defeat during the French and Indian War, the government of Louis XVI was not yet prepared to commit French soldiers to the support of the Americans. King Louis was looking for proof that the American army would be a strong ally that could stand up against the British in battle.

On December 4, 1777, Benjamin Franklin received a messenger from America. Franklin was now an elderly man of more than seventy, but his age did not reduce his vigorous efforts on behalf of the American government in trying to win over the French. Franklin had already heard rumors that the armies of General Washington

News of Burgoyne's surrender reached America's ambassador to France, Benjamin Franklin, in December, 1777. Two months later, the French signed a treaty to assist the United States in their war against Great Britain.

had suffered a defeat. "Is Philadelphia taken?" he asked the messenger almost immediately and was told that the American capital had indeed fallen. Franklin was very upset. The messenger continued: "But sir, I have greater news than that. General Burgoyne and his whole army are prisoners of war!" Franklin was jubilant.

This was the victory that Franklin had been awaiting. When news of it reached the French government, the impact was immediate. On December 17, 1777, Franklin was informed that Louis XVI had decided to recognize American independence and form an alliance with the new government. On February 6, 1778, the treaty was formally signed, and during the following month France declared war on Great Britain.

By June of 1778, French and English ships were engaged in battle off the European coast. The war would also spread to the Caribbean Sea, where Britain and France would battle each other for rich colonies. The entry of France into the war meant that the British could no longer concentrate their armies and navies in North America, trying to put down the revolution. Instead, English forces would have to be spread much thinner— between America, Europe, and the Caribbean. In the meantime, France began sending troops and ships to America, as well as more money and military supplies. These helped to support the American armies and keep them in the field where they continued to confront the English.

Eventually, in June 1778, the English forces evacuated Philadelphia and concentrated their armies in New York. Meanwhile, the British decided to invade the South, hoping that the large number of Tories reported to be there might rise up and join them. After some early victories, however, the British retreated to Virginia. There, in 1781, a British army under the command of General Charles Cornwallis, entrenched itself at Yorktown on the coast of Virginia. While Cornwallis was there, a combined French and American army marched to Virginia and besieged the British soldiers. Cornwallis hoped that an English fleet would rescue his army. However, the fleet was defeated off the coast by a French squadron.

The French alliance with the United States led to final victory against the British at Yorktown in 1781.

Almost exactly four years after Burgoyne's surrender at Saratoga, Cornwallis was forced to surrender at Yorktown. The alliance that had brought France into the war had led to a final victory in 1781 that secured American independence.

The road to Yorktown had begun at Saratoga, for without this victory, Yorktown would have been impossible. Saratoga was the turning point of the American Revolution.

1755	French begin construction of Fort Carillon
1759	British capture Fort Carillon, renaming it Fort Ticonderoga
	British capture Quebec
1760	Montreal falls to the British
1775	American Revolution begins with battles at Lexington and Concord
	Fort Ticonderoga captured by Americans
	Montreal captured by Americans
	American assault on Quebec is repulsed by British
1776	British capture New York City
	British win Battle of Valcour Island on Lake Champlain
1777	
June	Burgoyne leaves Canada to begin invasion of New York

1775
Montreal captured
by Americans

1776
British win Battle of
Valcour Island on
Lake Champlain

1775
American Revolution
begins with battles
at Lexington and
Concord

1776
American assault on
Quebec is repulsed
by British

1775

1776

1775
Fort Ticonderoga captured
by Americans

Timeline

July	British capture Fort Ticonderoga
	British General Fraser wins Battle of Hubbardtown
	Burgoyne captures Skenesborough
August	Americans win Battle of Bennington
	British lay siege to Fort Stanwix on Mohawk River
	Americans and British fight at Battle of Oriskany
	Siege of Fort Stanwix is lifted, and British retreat
September	British troops under General Howe defeat General Washington at Battle of Brandywine Creek near Philadelphia
	Americans and British fight at Battle of Freeman's Farm
	General Howe occupies Philadelphia
October	General Howe wins Battle of Germantown

June 1777
Burgoyne leaves Canada to begin invasion of New York

July 1777
British capture Fort Ticonderoga

British General Fraser wins Battle of Hubbardtown

Burgoyne captures Skenesborough

September 1777
Americans and British fight at Battle of Freeman's Farm

October 1777
Americans win decisive battle at Bemis Heights

British capture Fort Montgomery and Fort Clinton on Hudson River

General Burgoyne surrenders at Saratoga

February 1778
France signs formal treaty of alliance with Americans

France declares war on Great Britain

1777 **1778**

August 1777
Americans win Battle of Bennington

British lay siege to Fort Stanwix on Mohawk River

Americans and British fight at Battle of Oriskany

Siege of Fort Stanwix is lifted, and British retreat

December 1777
France recognizes American independence

Americans win decisive battle at Bemis Heights

British capture Fort Montgomery and Fort Clinton on Hudson River

General Burgoyne surrenders at Saratoga

December   France recognizes American independence

1778

February   France signs formal treaty of alliance with Americans

France declares war on Great Britain

June   British evacuate Philadelphia

1781   General Cornwallis surrenders at Yorktown

Billias, George Athan, ed. *George Washington's Generals.* New York: William Morrow, 1964.

Connell, Brian. *The Savage Years.* New York: Harper and Brothers, 1959.

Cook, Fred J. *Dawn Over Saratoga: The Turning Point of the Revolutionary War.* Garden City: Doubleday, 1973.

Flexner, James Thomas. *Mohawk Baronet: Sir William Johnson of New York.* New York: Harper and Brothers, 1959.

Furneaux, Rupert. *The Battle of Saratoga.* New York: Stein and Day, 1971.

Hibbert, Christopher. *Redcoats and Rebels: The American Revolution Through British Eyes.* New York: Norton, 1990.

Ketchum, Richard. *Saratoga: Turning Point of America's Revolutionary War.* New York: Henry Holt, 1997.

Koster, John. "Jane McCrea, remembered as a victim of American Indian brutality, may have died under different circumstances." *Military History,* June, 2000.

Lancaster, Bruce. *Ticonderoga: The Story of a Fort.* Boston: Houghton Mifflin, 1959.

Lunt, James. *John Burgoyne of Saratoga.* New York: Harcourt Brace Jovanovich, 1975.

Martin, James Kirby. *Benedict Arnold, Revolutionary Hero.* New York: New York University Press, 1997.

Moore, Howard. *The Life of General John Stark of New Hampshire.* Boston: Spaulding-Moss, 1949.

Scheer, George and Rankin, Hugh. *Rebels and Redcoats.* Cleveland: The World Publishing Company, 1957.

Ward, Christopher. *The War of The Revolution.* New York: Macmillan, 1952.

page:

2:   The New York Public Library
6:   © Bettmann/Corbis
11: © Francis G. Mayer/Corbis
14: © Bettmann/Corbis
18: Hulton Archive by Getty Images
20: © Francis G. Mayer/Corbis
23: The New York Public Library
24: Hulton Archive by Getty Images
26: © Bettmann/Corbis
28: © Lee Snider/Corbis
34: New York Historical Society
38: © Robert Holmes/Corbis
40: © Bettmann/Corbis
42: Hulton Archive by Getty Images
46: Scala/Art Resource, NY
49: Hulton Archive by Getty Images
51: © Lee Snider/Corbis
54: Hulton Archive by Getty Images
57: Hulton Archive by Getty Images

60: © Lee Snider/Corbis
63: Hulton Archive by Getty Images
65: Hulton Archive by Getty Images
68: National Portrait Gallery,
     Smithsonian
72: © Bettmann/Corbis
76: Hulton Archive by Getty Images
79: Scala/Art Resource, NY
80: © Bettmann/Corbis
82: Hulton Archive by Getty Images
87: Hulton Archive by Getty Images
91: Hulton Archive by Getty Images
92: New York Historical Society
94: © David Muench/Corbis
100: The New York Public Library
103: Architect of the Capitol
105: Hulton Archive by Getty Images
107: Hulton Archive by Getty Images

cover: Granger Collection

RICHARD WORTH has thirty years experience as a writer, trainer, and video producer. He has written more than 25 books, including *The Four Levers of Corporate Change*, a best-selling business book. Many of his books are for young adults on topics that include family living, foreign affairs, biography, history, and the criminal justice system.